PROPHECY AND RELIGION
IN ANCIENT CHINA
AND ISRAEL

The lectures here printed were originally delivered at the School of Oriental and African Studies of the University of London as the Louis H. Jordan Lectures in Comparative Religion for 1954. Three earlier volumes of the Jordan Lecture series are published in Great Britain by the Athlone Press.

Prophecy and Religion in Ancient China and Israel

By

H. H. ROWLEY

*Professor of Hebrew Language and Literature
in the University of Manchester*

HARPER & BROTHERS PUBLISHERS
NEW YORK

CONTENTS

ABBREVIATIONS

A.J.S.L.	*American Journal of Semitic Languages and Literatures.*
A.R.W.	*Archiv für Religionswissenschaft.*
B.A.S.O.R.	*Bulletin of the American Schools of Oriental Research.*
B.J.R.L.	*Bulletin of the John Rylands Library.*
D.B.	Hastings's *Dictionary of the Bible.*
E.R.E.	Hastings's *Encyclopaedia of Religion and Ethics.*
E.T.	*Expository Times.*
J.A.O.S.	*Journal of the American Oriental Society.*
J.B.L.	*Journal of Biblical Literature.*
J.T.S.	*Journal of Theological Studies.*
Ned.T.T.	*Nederlands Theologisch Tijdschrift.*
P.A.A.J.R.	*Proceedings of the American Academy for Jewish Research.*
R.Ass.	*Revue d'Assyriologie et d'Archéologie orientale.*
R.B.	*Revue Biblique.*
R.Th.Ph.	*Revue de Théologie et de Philosophie.*
Th.L.Z.	*Theologische Literaturzeitung.*
T.S.K.	*Theologische Studien und Kritiken.*
Z.A.W.	*Zeitschrift für die alttestamentliche Wissenschaft.*
Z.D.M.G.	*Zeitschrift der deutschen morgenländischen Gesellschaft.*

I

The Nature of Prophecy

WHEN I was honoured with the invitation to deliver the
Louis H. Jordan Bequest Lectures in Comparative
Religion at the School of Oriental and African Studies,
I readily accepted, despite a heavy burden of other commitments,
because it gave me an opportunity to bring together two fields
of study in which I have long been interested. The terms of the
invitation required me to bring together two religions, and of these
one is naturally the religion of Israel, in whose study I have been
professionally engaged for most of my working life. The other is
perhaps equally naturally the field of Chinese religion, in which I
was interested long before I went to live and work in China,
and in which I became more deeply interested through my resi-
dence there. The first supervisor of my Chinese studies was my
then next-door neighbour, Dr. J. Percy Bruce, who afterwards
became Professor of Chinese in this School, and who once urged
me to abandon my Semitic studies and to devote myself wholly to
Chinese. I was already too far committed for this, but I have retained through the years a close interest in things Chinese. That I
am not a specialist in this field as in the Old Testament field, however, I must at the outset confess. But it is hard for anyone to be a
real specialist in two such widely different fields, and since the
terms of the Louis H. Jordan Bequest require a comparison of
two fields, it is almost inevitable that the lecturer will be more of a
specialist in one than in the other.

I have chosen as my subject 'Prophecy and Religion in Ancient
China and Israel' because I believe that here we have a significant
point of comparison between the two fields. Few people think
of the Chinese Sages of the classical period alongside the Old

Testament prophets of the eighth, seventh and sixth centuries
B.C.,[1] and many think of the prophets of Israel as quite unique in
the history of religion. Such may expect that what I have to
say in these lectures will be just to contrast the Chinese Sages
with the prophets of Israel, to the detriment of the former. In
fact things are not quite so simple as that. It will be my aim neither
to obscure the real differences there were nor to exaggerate them.

E. R. Hughes has uttered a warning against making one of two
things which are being compared unconsciously the standard for
the other.[2] This is a danger to which we are all subject in our
comparisons, and to which I am especially exposed by the terms
of my subject. For prophecy is something intimately associated
in our thought with the Old Testament, whereas there are no
claims to a comparable prophetic character amongst the sages of
China. The Israelite prophets are playing on their home pitch
and start with a clear advantage. I shall strive, however, not to be
unfair to the Chinese teachers of whom I shall speak. Before we
can judge it is necessary to understand, and to place ourselves as
far as we can alongside men in their own times. Neither group of
teachers should be judged from the standpoint of the other, nor
even from our standpoint today. Superficial judgements are
always the easiest to make, and for most people they suffice. If
a figure from the past does not appeal to us as one we should want
to follow if he were transported across the ages to the present, we
do not hesitate to criticize him, without stopping to reflect that if
the leader we choose to follow today were transported into the
past he would cut a sorry figure. We ourselves are the creatures of
our own age to a far greater degree than we care to acknowledge,
and our thought and conduct is to a large extent conditioned by
the thought and conduct of our own time. None should be

[1] E. R. and K. Hughes (*Religion in China*, 1950, p. 29) say that Confucius is to
be regarded as a prophet such as we find in the Old Testament, and elsewhere
E. R. Hughes (*The Great Learning and the Mean-in-Action*, 1942, p. 74) describes
Mo-tzŭ as one who 'had a trenchant prophetic power about him, denounced the
evils of society without mincing matters, and in doing so was able to use a gift of
sarcasm with devastating effect'.

[2] Cf. *Chinese Philosophy in Classical Times*, 1942, p. xii.

condemned because he belonged to his own age and setting. Similarly we should recognize that if the Chinese Sages would not have fitted well into the life of Ancient Israel, it is highly improbable that the Israelite prophets would have appeared other than exotic in Ancient China.

It is necessary first to indicate what I mean by prophecy, and to guard against a definition which prejudges the issues. Many people understand the term to mean prediction of the future, and not a few think of it primarily in terms of the prediction of the distant future. There are many who term themselves students of prophecy who mean that they endeavour to find out by means of the study of the Bible what will happen in our day and our children's day. The history of such study is strewn with disappointments.[1] It is unnecessary to say that in these lectures I am not thinking of prophecy in that sense, if only because there are none who treat the records of the Chinese Sages so, and no helpful comparison could be made along those lines.

Against such an approach to the Old Testament prophets others revolt so strongly that they are not interested in these men as predictors of the future at all, and an oft-repeated dictum is that the prophets were not foretellers but forthtellers.[2] This antithesis seems to me to be quite misleading. For the Old Testament prophets were both forthtellers and foretellers. Again and again they did predict the future,[3] both the immediate future that should arise out of the conditions of their own times, and the more distant future on the far horizons of time.[4] I would not eliminate the predictive element in prophecy; on the other hand I would not let it crowd out the other elements.

[1] Cf. R. B. Y. Scott, *The Relevance of the Prophets*, 1944, p. 3.

[2] Cf. R. H. Charles, *Critical and Exegetical Commentary on the Book of Daniel*, 1929, p. xxvi: 'Prophecy is a declaration, a forthtelling, of the will of God—not a foretelling. Prediction is not in any sense an essential element of prophecy, though it may intervene as an accident.'

[3] Cf. R. B. Y. Scott, *op. cit.*, p. 9: 'There remains in their (i.e. the great prophets') prophecy an element of prediction which it is important to distinguish from the prognostications of the soothsayers and diviners.'

[4] Cf. what I have written in *The Rediscovery of the Old Testament*, 1946, pp. 203, 184.

The Hebrew word for prophecy has no connotation of prediction.[1] While its real meaning is disputed, it is quite certain that the fundamental meaning of the word has nothing to do with prediction. There are some who think the term has reference to the ecstatic behaviour of the prophet,[2] because an associated verbal form certainly means *to act like one beside himself.*[3] It is used of Saul when he hurled javelins at the people about him.[4] There can be no doubt that the prophets sometimes acted in strange ways. When Saul was caught up into a prophetic spirit he tore his clothes off and rolled about naked.[5] If the essence of prophecy were to be found here, it would be vain to essay any comparison with the Chinese teachers. For nothing is harder to imagine than Confucius behaving thus. It is probable, however, that the verbal form in Hebrew is a denominative from the noun which means *prophet*, and that it simply means *to act like a prophet*. It does not give us, therefore, the primary, etymological meaning of the word *nābhî'*.[6] There are others who associate the Hebrew word with an Accadian word *nabû*, which means *call*, and think it has reference to the call, or vocation, of the prophet,[7] or to the fact of his calling, or proclaiming, his message.[8] While this view is probably correct, etymology cannot suffice for our purpose. The

[1] I have discussed this more fully in *The Servant of the Lord*, 1952, pp. 96 ff., where references to much recent literature on the nature of Hebrew prophecy may be found.

[2] Cf. J. Pedersen, *Israel III–IV*, 1940, p. 111; 'The term *nābhî'* is perhaps derived from the ecstatic incoherent cries.' Cf. also T. H. Robinson, in *The Expositor*, 8th series, xxi, 1921, p. 224.

[3] Cf. 1 Sam. xix. 24; also 1 Kings xviii. 28.

[4] Cf. 1 Sam. xviii. 10, where the R.V. translates 'prophesied', but in the margin adds 'Or, raved.'

[5] 1 Sam. xix. 24.

[6] J. A. Bewer, *A.J.S.L.*, xviii, 1901–2, p. 120, attempted to provide this etymological meaning by connecting the Hebrew word *nābhî'* with the Accadian *nabû* = *tear away*, and thought the primary significance of the Hebrew word was *one who is carried away by a supernatural power*.

[7] Cf. H. Torczyner, *Z.D.M.G.*, lxxxv, 1931, p. 322; W. F. Albright, *From the Stone Age to Christianity*, 2nd ed., 1946, pp. 231 f.

[8] Cf. F. Häussermann, *Wortempfang und Symbol in der alttestamentlichen Propheten*, 1932, p. 10; E. König, *Hebräisches und aramäisches Wörterbuch zum Alten Testament*, 1936 ed., p. 260 b.

Hebrew prophets—at least the greater prophets with whom we shall be concerned—were conscious of a divine call to their ministry, and we read references to the dramatic experiences whereby some of them received this call. We know something of the call of Amos,[1] Isaiah,[2] Jeremiah,[3] and Ezekiel.[4] The call of Hosea came through a long and painful experience,[5] though it may well have begun in a dramatic moment when he realized that he must marry Gomer.[6] Wheeler Robinson has surmised that no Hebrew prophet would venture to prophesy without an initial experience of an extraordinary character.[7] Of the Chinese Sages we have no record of similar memorable experiences in which they heard the voice of God summoning them to their task, though they were not without the consciousness that their mission had been laid upon them. Confucius could say 'After the death of King Wên, was not the cause of truth lodged here in me?'[8] Similarly when Mencius heard that he was charged with

[1] Amos vii. 14 f.

[2] Isa. vi.

[3] Jer. i. 4 ff.

[4] Ezek. i.

[5] The story of Hosea's marriage is of perennial interest to scholars, and agreement about it seems unlikely ever to be reached. For a summary survey of the views propounded cf. *The Servant of the Lord*, p. 115 n.

[6] Hos. i. 2.

[7] Cf. *Redemption and Revelation*, 1942, pp. 143 f. Cf. also J. P. Hyatt, *Prophetic Religion*, 1947, p. 17.

[8] *Analects* IX, v, Legge's translation (*The Chinese Classics*, i, 2nd ed., 1893, p. 217). There is in the Chinese a play on words here, since what Legge renders by *the cause of truth* is the single word *wên*, identical with the name of King Wên. That word is more usually found in the meaning *literature* or *culture*, and W. E. Soothill (*The Analects of Confucius*, 1910, p. 423) renders 'Since King Wên is no longer alive, does not (the mantle of) enlightenment rest here on me?' With this cf. the rendering of H. O. H. Stange, *Gedanken und Gespräche des Konfuzius*, 1953, p. 88. L. A. Lyall (*The Sayings of Confucius*, 3rd ed., 1953, p. 37) has 'Since the death of King Wên, is not the seat of culture here?' With this cf. A. Waley, *The Analects of Confucius*, 1938, p. 139: 'When King Wên perished, did that mean that culture ceased to exist?' For his unusual rendering of *wên* by *the cause of truth* here, Legge follows the view that Confucius used *wên* instead of *tao* through modesty. For our purpose the precise rendering of this word is immaterial, since the context clearly indicates the Sage's conviction that the cause of truth, or enlightenment, or culture, was entrusted to him by Heaven.

being fond of disputing, he replied 'I am not fond of disputing, but I am compelled to do it.'[1] Certainly I am not disposed to question that the Chinese Sages were raised up by God, though the form of their experience was doubtless very different from that of the Hebrew prophets. But they were not public preachers, as the Israelite prophets appear to have been. Their methods were, as we shall see, in many respects quite different from those of the Hebrew figures whom we shall study. It seems to me, however, quite unsatisfactory to define prophecy in terms of its forms of expression. For its essential nature we need to penetrate more deeply.

Professor Guillaume has argued that the meaning of the Hebrew word *nābhî'* is *one who is in the state of announcing a message which has been given to him*.[2] Whether this is the etymological meaning of the term or not is not of primary importance to us, since a comparison of Hebrew and Chinese figures can hardly be governed by a question of Hebrew etymology. The definition will, however, serve for our purpose. If we regard the Chinese Sages as in any sense the mouthpiece of God they fall within this definition of prophecy, which leaves unspecified the ways in which they exercised their function. Both Hebrew prophets and Chinese Sages spoke primarily to their own age a word that was relevant to the conditions of their day. If the sayings of both prophets and sages are still cherished, it is because they have been found also to speak a word that has a wider relevance than that to their own age. But neither can be understood unless first studied in the light of their times. An essential part of the word in the case of the Old Testament prophets was the warning of the issue of the policies

---

[1] *Mencius* III Part 2, ix. 1, 13. For translations of Mencius cf. J. Legge, *The Chinese Classics*, ii, 2nd ed., 1895; S. Couvreur, *Les Quatre Livres*, 2nd ed., 1910; M. G. Pauthier, *Doctrine de Confucius*; L. A. Lyall, *Mencius*, 1932; R. Wilhelm, *Mong Dsi*, 1921. Where a translation is cited in the text, Legge's rendering will normally be given.

[2] Cf. *Prophecy and Divination*, 1938, pp. 112 f. Cf. also G. C. Aalders, *De Profeten des Ouden Verbonds*, 1918, p. 11; 'De naam *nabi*' beteekent *Spreker die het woord van God vertolkt.*' J. Paterson (*The Goodly Fellowship of the Prophets*, 1948, p. 3) similarly defines the prophet as one who speaks by delegated authority.

that were being pursued, and of the consequences of the social and moral conditions of their times. But surely the same can be said of Mencius, in particular.

This definition leaves on one side mere prediction of the future *qua* prediction. Other peoples and other ages have been eager to know the future, and the prophets of Israel are not the only persons to whom men have turned to secure such knowledge on either private or public affairs. Diviners of various kinds were known in the ancient world, and the references to them in the Old Testament show that they were not unknown amongst the Israelites.[1] Joseph is said to have used a cup for divination, in a context where no censure would seem to be implied.[2] But usually all forms of necromancy and divination, which sought to discover the future, as well as all forms of spells which sought to control the future, are rejected and condemned.[3] Necromancers and diviners and magicians were mere technicians who professed to be able to discover the future by their skill, or to determine it by their spells. The modern students of prophecy, who suppose that they can foretell the future by the minute study of Daniel and the Apocalypse, are as much diviners as their ancient counterparts who claimed to be able to foretell the future by examining the liver of animals or by watching the flight of birds. Both sup-

---

[1] Cf. Isa. iii. 2, Mic. iii. 11, Jer. xxvii. 9, xxix. 8, where diviners are mentioned alongside prophets in a way that indicates that some prophets were diviners. Cf. also Ezek. xiii. 6, 9, xxii. 28. On divination cf. T. Witton Davies, *Magic, Divination and Demonology among the Hebrews and their Neighbours*, 1898.

[2] Gen. xliv. 2, 5.

[3] Cf. Lev. xix. 26, Deut. xviii. 10, 1 Sam. xv. 23, xxviii. 3, 2 Kings xvii. 17, xxi. 6. Divination by Urim and Thummim took place in early times, but later seems to have fallen into desuetude, Urim and Thummim becoming mere elements of the High Priest's equipment. The Septuagint rendering of 1 Sam. xiv. 41 is the most important surviving passage for the discussion of their use, though this passage does not tell us what they were, or how they were used. It seems most probable that they were two flat stones, each with an auspicious side, *tummîm*, and an inauspicious side, *'ûrîm*, giving an auspicious answer to the question posed if both showed the auspicious side, and an inauspicious answer if both showed the inauspicious side, but giving no answer at all if each showed a different side. Cf. H. Doré, *Recherches sur les superstitions en Chine*, I, ii (Variétés sinologiques, No. 34), 1912, p. 243, where a similar device used in Chinese divination is described.

pose that the knowledge they seek has been divinely hidden, and that by a right technique they can discover it. The repeated condemnation of all forms of divination in the Old Testament, within the prophetic books as well as without,[1] makes it very hard to accept the view that the Hebrew prophets should be equated with various Babylonian orders of priests, who were technicians in divination, either by hepatoscopy or by some other specialized technique. Such a view has been propounded,[2] but it is certainly not to be accepted so far as the Hebrew prophets whom we shall consider are concerned.

Similarly China was not without diviners. There are evidences of divination long before the time of Confucius,[3] and one of the Confucian Classics, the *I Ching*, is a book of divination.[4] Taoism has become associated with divination and magic. James Legge writes 'Every member of the order has his own ability, and makes more or less by writing charms and preparing amulets.'[5] And again: 'The aim of the Taoists is especially to provide the proper spots for the graves. Only adepts in the system can be relied on to do this, and large sums are often paid for their services.'[6] As for Mo-

---

[1] The references to the diviners in the prophetic books associate them with the false prophets who are repudiated; cf. Jer. xxvii. 9, xxix. 8, Ezek. xiii. 6, 9, Zech. x. 2.

[2] Cf. A. Haldar, *Associations of Cult Prophets among the Ancient Semites*, 1945, where Hebrew prophecy is seen in terms of the *bārū* and *maḫḫū* guilds of Babylonia. M. Bič (*V.T.*, i, 1951, pp. 293 ff.) holds that Amos was a *hepatoscopos*. Against this cf. A. Murtonen (*ibid.*, ii, 1952, pp. 170 f.).

[3] Cf. E. R. Hughes, *op. cit.*, p. 7; 'Study of the Yen Oracles and of the earliest surviving books reveals that divination plays a very important part in early Chinese religion.' Cf. also H. A. Giles, *Confucianism and its Rivals*, 1915, pp. 25 f. In the *Shu Ching* V, Book 4, iii. 20 ff., divination by tortoise and milfoil is enjoined. For the *Shu Ching*, cf. J. Legge, *The Chinese Classics*, iii, 2 vols., 1865, or S. Couvreur, *Chou Ching*, 1916. On the method of divination by the tortoise, as indicated by surviving oracular bones, cf. R. Wilhelm, *A Short History of Chinese Civilization*, E. Tr. by Joan Joshua, 1929, p. 85.

[4] E. R. Hughes, *op. cit.*, p. 8, says: 'By the time Confucius lived this book, in its earliest unamplified form, had attained high religious sanctity.' On the *I Ching* cf. A. Forke, *Geschichte der alten chinesischen Philosophie*, 1927, pp. 9 ff. R. Wilhelm's translation of the *I Ching* has now been rendered into English by C. F. Baynes, 2 vols., 1951.

[5] *The Religions of China*, 1850, p. 198.   [6] *Ibid.*, pp. 199 f.

tzŭ, it would seem that we owe the preservation of his works to Taoists who were only interested in some alchemy which they found in them. H. R. Williamson says: 'Throughout a period of more than sixteen hundred years the Taoists preserved the writings of this ancient sage, for the simple reason that they found in them a quite negligible amount of alchemistic knowledge which appealed to them.'[1] Yet we cannot think of Confucius, or the founder of Taoism, or Mo-tzŭ, as diviners. Of Confucius E. R. and K. Hughes say: 'Critical scholarship to-day has every reason to doubt whether he (i.e. Confucius) paid any attention to the compilation (the I Ching) as it was in his day, or had any particular interest in divination.'[2] Similarly H. A. Giles had earlier said: 'In the intimate conversations of Confucius with his disciples we do not come across any direct reference to divination; but from an essay composed by his grandson and disciple we learn that the reeds and the tortoise-shell were still employed.'[3]

There is, however, a good deal of evidence that Old Testament prophets were consulted, both on matters of state and on private matters, in the effort to discover the future, or to give wise guidance for the present. Saul went to Ramah to consult Samuel about his father's lost asses.[4] Jeroboam sent his wife to consult Ahijah as to whether his son would recover.[5] Hezekiah sent for Isaiah in a time of crisis to know what he should do.[6] Ahab sent for a host of prophets to forecast the issue of the projected war with the northern state of Damascus.[7] That there is here something akin to divination is clear. In all these cases there was the desire to get access to knowledge that was not available to men naturally. By what technique the prophet found the answer we do not know, and it may be that he relied entirely on inner illumination. Professor Guillaume has brought forward many parallels to this sort of prophecy from Arabia, and has discussed the methods by which

[1] Mo Ti: a Chinese Heretic, 1927, pp. 10 f.
[2] Religion in China, 1950, p. 47. In the Chia Yü II, 17b, Sect. x, §3 (R. P. Kramers, K'ung Tzŭ Chia Yü, 1950, p. 244) Confucius is said to have divined for himself, but on the Chia Yü see below, p. 100 n.
[3] Confucianism and its Rivals, p. 79.   [4] 1 Sam. ix. 6.
[5] 1 Kings xiv. 1 ff.   [6] 2 Kings xix. 2.   [7] 1 Kings xxii. 6.

the answers to such questions were obtained.[1] Sometimes some object on which the eye by chance fell would suggest the answer. Here we are reminded of the way in which some of the oracles of Amos and Jeremiah took their origin. Although they were not answers to questions put to them, they arose out of visual experiences. Amos saw a man with a plumbline[2] and this led him to think of the Divine test to which men were being subjected.[3] Jeremiah saw a cauldron boiling over and thought of the cauldron of Israel.[4] Or again he saw a potter at work, and this suggested to him the analogous activity of God in human affairs.[5] Sometimes it was by curious word plays in their minds that they found their message. Amos saw a basket of summer fruit, and his mind sprang from the word *ḳaiṣ*, rendered *summer fruit*, to the word *ḳēṣ*, which means *end*, and the basket of fruit supplied only the occasion and not the content of his message.[6] Similarly Jeremiah saw an almond tree in blossom, and his thought travelled from the word *shāḳēdh*, or *almond tree*, to *shōḳēdh*, or *waking*, and to God's attitude to the affairs of Israel.[7] While in none of these cases does the prophetic word come in answer to some question submitted to the prophet,[8] and they are thus differentiated from the other cases just mentioned, it may well have been that the answers to the questions were sometimes found in comparable ways.

None of this is of serious concern to us in these lectures, since we do not find anything comparable with this amongst the Chinese Sages who will come before us. It is true that Mencius was sometimes consulted on affairs of state, as some of the Israelite prophets were on occasion. Thus King Hsüan asked him whether he should

---

[1] Cf. *Prophecy and Divination*, 1938, pp. 117 ff.

[2] A. Condamin, *R.B.*, ix, 1900, pp. 586 ff., argued that the Septuagint here correctly understood the Hebrew to mean *adamant*, and that the picture was of one with a sword in his hand. J. Morgenstern, *Amos Studies*, i, 1941, p. 83, defends the more usual view, and so V. Maag, *Text, Wortschatz und Begriffswelt des Buches Amos*, 1951, p. 66.

[3] Amos vii. 7 ff.   [4] Jer. i. 13 ff.   [5] Jer. xviii. 1 ff.
[6] Amos viii. 1 ff.   [7] Jer. i. 11 f.

[8] Most of the predictions of the future found in the prophetic books arise from the inner initiative of the prophets, an initiative which they believed to be due to the direct working of the spirit of God within them.

conquer Yen,[1] and Duke Wên whether he should serve one or the other of his more powerful neighbours.[2] But there is no suggestion that Mencius employed supernatural powers, or gave answer save as human wisdom determined. There is no reason to suppose that he was thought to employ a technique akin in any way to divination, or to receive some special *ad hoc* illumination.

It is clear, therefore, that if any profitable comparison is to be made, we must concentrate on certain features of the Hebrew prophets and of the Chinese Sages that lend themselves to comparison, and that other features must be left out of account. It must therefore be observed that I do not wish to give the impression that the features to be considered were the only ones to be found in either group of teachers. So far as the Israelite prophets were concerned, it must be remembered that there were many varieties, and that deep inner divisions were to be found amongst them. Jeremiah denounces false prophets,[3] and it is clear that they regarded Jeremiah as a false prophet.[4] He classes them with diviners and dreamers and dismisses them with contempt.[5] The first occasion on which we have clear evidence of this inner division amongst the prophets is the already mentioned eve of the attack on the Damascus state by Ahab.[6] All the prophets with the single exception of Micaiah encouraged him to make the attack and promised him victory, while Micaiah warned him against the enterprise. The event here proved that Micaiah was a true prophet and the others false prophets; but it was not always so easy to establish the distinction. Nor was it of any help to Ahab to have the distinction established after he had paid with his life for his trust in the delusive word. When the book of Deuteronomy tries to lay down canons for the detection of false prophecy, it cannot do so very satisfactorily though it tries twice. In one place it lays it down that the prophet whose word did not come true was not a true prophet of Yahweh.[7] But this offered

---

[1] *Mencius* I Part 2, x. 2.
[2] *Mencius* I Part 2, xiii. 1.
[3] Jer. xxiii. 9 ff., xxvii. 14 ff.
[4] Cf. Jer. xxviii. 10 f.
[5] Jer. xxvii. 9.
[6] 1 Kings xxii.
[7] Deut. xviii. 22.

men no means of distinguishing at the time when the prophecy was uttered, and therefore gave no guidance to perplexed people who heard two rival voices. In the other place, Deuteronomy lays it down that any prophet who sought to lead men away from Yahweh was a false prophet.[1] But this, again, did not get men far. The prophets to whom Ahab so disastrously listened claimed to be prophets of Yahweh, and were not leading the king away from Him. The difference between the true prophet and the false prophet was one which could only be spiritually discerned, and the predictive element in prophecy was not its only criterion. All the Hebrew prophets, of whatever variety and however opposed they might be to one another, claimed to bring an authoritative word of God to men, and to offer Divine guidance in the affairs of their day, either public or private, or both.

The study of Hebrew prophecy, then, is no simple study, and the phenomenon of prophecy is more complex than we like to suppose. If there were great men, such as Amos and Hosea, Isaiah and Jeremiah, and Deutero-Isaiah, to name no others, men who brought a dynamic word of God to men, and who were figures of importance in the religious history of Israel, it must be remembered that they stood out from a background of others. When we talk of the uniqueness of Old Testament prophecy, we must be careful not to suppose that the whole institution of Israelite prophecy was unlike anything that could be found amongst any other people. The uniqueness is found only in the heights that were attained. Just as the uniqueness of Everest is in the fact that it is the highest mountain in the world, and not in that it is the only mountain, so the uniqueness of the great prophets of Israel is to be found in the heights they attained. They were not the only Israelite prophets, and it is impossible to draw any sharp lines of division between them and the other prophets, to mark them off as of a different kind. One of the stories which I find most instructive as a warning against any simple classification of the Old Testament prophets is the story of the prophet from Judah who prophesied at Bethel against Jeroboam I.[2] He stands

[1] Deut. xiii. 1 ff. (Heb. 2 ff.).   [2] 1 Kings xiii.

before us as a man of God, fearless and inspired. Yet he is misled by the delusive word of the old prophet into returning to Bethel to eat with him, though he had earlier declared that by Divine illumination he had learned that he was not to eat in Bethel. Where an authentic prophet could not distinguish the true prophet from the false, how could ordinary folk be expected to do so? Moreover, the old prophet who gave as a word of God the delusive word that was rooted in his own will stands before us as a false prophet. Yet a little later he announces to the man whom he has deluded the authentic word of God, rebuking him for his disobedience and predicting the heavy penalty he should pay. The man who is one minute a false prophet is a true prophet the next.

It is also impossible to mark off Israel's prophets as different in kind from the prophets of other peoples. The Old Testament presents us with Balaam,[1] who is clearly represented as a non-Israelite person comparable with the prophets of Israel. It is true that he was summoned to curse Israel, and that it was supposed that his word would have power to effect its own fulfilment, but that unexpectedly he was moved by God to bless instead of curse. It is easy to dismiss Balaam and the man who engaged him as believers in magic, and in the power of the curse. But widely in the Old Testament we find the belief in the power of blessings and curses, and genuine prophets could pronounce vigorous curses on those who opposed them. Amos could prophesy against Amaziah in terms that were indistinguishable from a curse,[2] and it was to pronounce such words against Israel that Balak summoned Balaam. We should not forget that every prophetic word was believed to have a vitality within itself to work for its own fulfilment.[3] The prophet's word was not merely a forecast of the future. It was a living force which helped to mould the future. If it was not merely the prophet's own word, but God's, as he claimed, then it must be thought to be a word of power. That was why Ahab was so concerned at the ill-omened word of Micaiah, that he saw all Israel as sheep without a shepherd. By this word

<hr>

[1] Num. xxii ff.   [2] Amos vii. 17.   [3] Cf. Isa. xlv. 23, lv. 10 f.

Micaiah was not merely forecasting the death of Ahab, but helping to bring it about.[1] Had it been merely a forecast, there would
have been no need to imprison Micaiah. It was because Micaiah
had released a force hostile to the king that he was imprisoned, and
the king took every precaution to defeat his hostile word. He
disguised himself and let Jehoshaphat wear his robes. It is often
thought that Jehoshaphat must have felt this to be a dangerous
honour, especially since it was the sequel to Micaiah's word. But
since Micaiah's word had not been directed against Jehoshaphat
he was in no way threatened by it. Ahab knew that he alone was
threatened, and he wished to minimize the threat by making
himself inconspicuous in the eyes of the enemy. But clearly he
took Micaiah's word seriously as a potent word, releasing
hostile energy. In the same way Balaam's word was believed to be
charged with power, and that was why Balak was disturbed when
he uttered the word that was not desired. But Balaam was a
prophet in the same sense as many prophets in Israel.

So, again, the prophets of Baal, who were ranged against
Elijah on Mount Carmel,[2] were comparable with many Israelite
prophets. They danced about and gashed themselves with knives[3]
in behaviour that has come to be termed ecstatic.[4] But it has to be
remembered that when Saul was caught up into the spirit of
prophecy, he rolled about on the ground naked all night.[5] There
can be no doubt whatever that Israelite prophets were often
ecstatic, though I do not go so far as some and hold that the prophet was essentially and always ecstatic, and that his message came
to him invariably in the ecstatic state.[6] The verb which I have

---

[1] Cf. J. Pedersen, *Israel I–II*, 1926, p. 167: 'When an Israelite pronounces blessings on another, then these are not empty though kindly wishes for the future.
With the words: Thou art blessed! and: Thou art cursed! he has created a blessing
or a curse in his soul, and laid it into that of the other.'

[2] 1 Kings xviii. 19 ff.   [3] 1 Kings xviii. 28.

[4] H. W. Robinson (*Redemption and Revelation*, 1942, p. 140) criticizes the use of
the word *ecstatic*, and prefers to use the word *abnormal*; but the word is too firmly
established to be dislodged.   [5] 1 Sam. xix. 23 f.

[6] Cf. H. W. Robinson, in *The People and the Book* (ed. by A. S. Peake), 1925,
p. 373; J. P. Hyatt, *Prophetic Religion*, 1947, p. 17. For the contrary view cf. T. H.
Robinson, *Prophecy and the Prophets*, p. 50.

already mentioned, which is probably a denominative from the Hebrew name for a prophet, would not have come to mean not merely *to behave like a prophet*, but *to act like one beside himself*, if that was not how prophets frequently behaved. The prophet who anointed Jehu was referred to by Jehu's fellow officers as a mad-man,[1] and there was clearly not much to differentiate the beha-viour of many a prophet from the behaviour of the madman. Zedekiah, the son of Chenaanah, who led the prophets supporting Ahab's fatal adventure, came into the king's presence wearing horns of iron, and crying 'With these thou shalt gore the Syrians.'[2] It is certain that in our modern world he would quickly be dubbed a madman. Even Isaiah could walk the streets of Jerusalem naked and barefoot,[3] and Jeremiah could appear in the Temple wearing a wooden yoke.[4] All of these strange acts are examples not merely of abnormal behaviour, but of prophetic symbolism,[5] whereby the prophet released power by act instead of by word. To the Hebrew act and word were not so sharply distinguished as by us. The same term stood for both word and deed, and the prophet prophesied by act as well as by word.

All this has long been recognized and Israelite prophecy in its roots has been set in a background of Near Eastern prophecy and not studied in isolation. The ancient Egyptian story of Wen Amon brought its evidence of prophecy akin to Israelite prophecy already in the eleventh century B.C., at Byblos.[6] We read that a youth became possessed and continued in this state throughout the night, declaring that he was the mouthpiece of his god. J. A. Wilson says that 'the determinative of the word "(prophetically) possessed" shows a human figure in violent motion or epileptic convulsion'.[7] Here we have behaviour similar to that of ecstatic

---

[1] 2 Kings ix. 11.   [2] 1 Kings xxii. 11.

[3] Isa. xx. 3.   [4] Jer. xxvii. 2.

[5] Cf. H. W. Robinson, in *Old Testament Essays*, 1927, pp. 1 ff.; G. Fohrer, *Die symbolischen Handlungen der Propheten*, 1953.

[6] For a translation of the story cf. A. Erman, *The Literature of the Ancient Egyptians*, E. Tr. by A. M. Blackman, 1927, pp. 174 ff., or J. B. Pritchard's *Ancient Near Eastern Texts*, 1950, pp. 25 ff. (E. Tr. from the Egyptian by J. A. Wilson).

[7] *Ibid.*, p. 26 b n.

prophecy, and it is clear that the roots of prophecy must be set far back in the past. It was no new phenomenon when it comes before us at the time of the foundation of the monarchy, which was not far from the age in which the story of Wen Amon is set.

Many years ago T. H. Robinson conjectured that this kind of prophecy took its rise in Asia Minor, and from there spread to Syria and Palestine, and also into Greece.[1] From classical sources we have stories of similar behaviour, and the Delphic priestess is brought by him into association with the same range of conduct.[2] Professor Robinson ventured the suggestion that it was amongst the Hittites that this kind of prophecy had its origin.[3]

In recent years new material bearing on this question has come to light. For from the ancient Mari, which has yielded such remarkable finds, comes evidence of prophecy comparable with Israelite prophecy, long before the time of Wen Amon.[4] The emphasis here is not on the behaviour of the prophet but on the divinely given word which he declares. It would appear that the message came by divine initiative, and not in response to a question, as in some of the Old Testament cases at which we have looked. From Mari comes a case of divine illumination through the medium of a dream.[5] To this source of inspiration we have references also in the Old Testament,[6] and there are cases where revelation is given through dreams to others than prophets, though they are not always able to understand them without help.[7]

For the full understanding of Israelite prophecy, therefore, all of this and a great deal more must be borne constantly in mind. The origins of prophecy lie far back in the past, and the pheno-

---

[1] *Prophecy and the Prophets*, 1923, p. 33 f.

[2] Cf. *The Classical Quarterly*, xi, 1917, pp. 201 ff.

[3] *Prophecy and the Prophets*, p. 34.

[4] Cf. A. Lods, in *Studies in Old Testament Prophecy* (T. H. Robinson Festschrift, ed. by H. H. Rowley), 1950, pp. 103 ff., M. Noth, *B.J.R.L.*, xxxii, 1949–50, pp. 194 ff., and *Geschichte und Gotteswort im Alten Testament*, 1950, F. M. Th. de Liagre Böhl, in *Ned.T.T.*, iv, 1949–50, pp. 82 ff., W. von Soden, *Die Welt des Orients*, 1950, pp. 397 ff., and H. Schmökel, *Th.L.Z.*, lxxvi, 1951, cols. 54 ff.

[5] Cf. G. Dossin, *R.Ass.*, xlii, 1948, pp. 125 ff.

[6] Cf. Num. xii. 6, Jer. xxiii. 25 ff.   [7] Cf. Gen. xx. 3, xl. 5 ff., xli. 1 ff.

menon was not confined to Israel. There were prophets of many kinds and on many levels, and their behaviour was often odd and undignified. If I do not deal at length with all these things here, it is because there is no direct counterpart of them in China. There is no known general background out of which the Chinese Sages sprang comparable with what I have briefly described of the background of Israelite prophecy. It is hard to think of Confucius behaving like the ecstatic prophets, or even like Isaiah and Jeremiah in the incidents I have referred to. To him propriety was of vast importance, and in every situation he behaved with complete restraint. In the tenth book of the Analects we have a collection of traditions about him which make this abundantly clear.[1] He would not sit down unless his mat was straight,[2] or eat meat which was not cut properly.[3] In bed he did not lie like a corpse[4] or open his mouth in speech.[5] When he was about to mount his carriage, he stood erect and held the cord.[6] It is true that Chuang-tzŭ was no slave to propriety, and behaved in ways which seemed odd to his contemporaries. When his wife died, a visitor who came to condole with him was shocked to find him squatting on the ground, drumming and singing.[7] But it is a far cry from this to

---

[1] A. Waley (*The Analects of Confucius*, p. 21) says this book 'is a compilation of maxims from works on ritual', while E. R. Hughes (*Chinese Philosophy in Classical Times*, p. 15 n.) notes that here 'the desire to make a sage of him (i.e. Confucius) is very apparent. He is portrayed in all sorts of stained-glass attitudes.' A. Forke, *Geschichte der alten chinesischen Philosophie*, p. 110) appears to accept this book as authentic.

[2] *Analects* X, ix. The following translations of the Analects may be consulted: J. Legge, *The Chinese Classics*, i, 2nd ed., 1893; W. E. Soothill, *The Analects of Confucius*, 1910 (the translation is reprinted without the Chinese text or notes in *The Analects or the Conversations of Confucius*, 1937); L. A. Lyall, *The Sayings of Confucius*, 3rd ed., 1935; A. Waley, *The Analects of Confucius*, 1938; S. Couvreur, *Les Quatre Livres*, 1910, M. G. Pauthier, *Doctrine de Confucius*; R. Wilhelm, *Kung Futse Gespräche*, 1923; H. O. H. Stange, *Gedanken und Gespräche des Konfuzius*, 1953.   [3] *Analects* X, viii. 3.   [4] *Analects* X, xvi. 1.

[5] *Analects* X, viii. 9.   [6] *Analects* X, xvii. 1.

[7] *Chuang-tzŭ* xviii. 2. For translations of *Chuang-tzŭ* cf. J. Legge, *Sacred Books of the East*, xxxix and xl, 1891; H. A. Giles, *Chuang Tzŭ*, 1926; L. Wieger, *Taoïsme*, ii, 1913, pp. 209 ff. (with Chinese text). The references to Chuang-tzŭ will be given according to Legge's edition, and where translations are given in the text, Legge's rendering will normally be used.

ecstatic prophecy. It is a far cry indeed from Chuang-tzŭ to any-thing that can be called Old Testament prophecy, and he is not one of the Chinese figures we shall particularly study.[1] To return to Confucius, though he attached the greatest importance to words, he gives no indication of such an attitude to the spoken word as is found in Israel. It was not that he saw in words a living force able to control events. The power of his words was but their power to influence men. His sense of the importance of words sprang from their influence over men, and through men over events. He was concerned to rectify names, because men deceived themselves by false names.[2] It was the logical and psychological importance of precision in terms which impressed him.

To deal in any detail with all the Hebrew prophets and with all the Chinese Sages of the classical period would require far more time than I have in these lectures, and I must therefore limit myself to a few of the greater figures, and to aspects of their work and teaching in which they can fairly be compared. Of the Hebrew prophets I shall think mainly of the prophets of the eighth and seventh centuries B.C., though with some reference to others. Of

---

[1] Of the brilliance of Chuang-tzŭ as a satirist there can be no doubt. Ssŭ-ma Ch'ien in the *Shih Chi* lxiii, says 'His literary and dialectic skill was such that the best scholars of the age proved unable to refute his destructive criticism of the Confucian and Mihist schools' (translation of H. A. Giles, *Chuang Tzŭ*, p. viii). In the sub-title of his book *Chuang Tzŭ*, Giles calls this teacher *Mystic, Moralist and Social Reformer*, but I find little of the moral earnestness of the reformer. Ssŭ-ma Ch'ien (*loc. cit.*) narrates that a prince sent messengers to him, with costly gifts, and invited him to become Prime Minister, whereupon Chuang-tzŭ replied: 'You offer me great wealth and a proud position indeed; but have you never seen a sacrificial ox? When after being fattened up for several years, it is decked with embroidered trappings and led to the altar, would it not willingly then change places with some uncared-for pigling? . . . Begone! Defile me not! I would rather disport myself to my own enjoyment in the mire than be slave to the ruler of a State. I will never take office. Thus I shall remain free to follow my own inclina-tions' (translation of Giles, *loc. cit.*; cf. also *Chuang-tzŭ* xvii. 11, xxxii. 13). No true prophet was concerned for his own ease and comfort.

[2] Cf. *Analects* XIII, iii. A. Waley (*The Analects of Confucius*, p. 22) rejects this as inauthentic. Indeed he does not appear to think that many authentic sayings of Confucius have been preserved at all (cf. p. 25). A. Forke rates it more highly. He says (*op. cit.*, p. 117): 'Fast alle Chinesen halten die Aussprüche des Confuzius, wie sie uns das *Lun-yü* darbietet, für authentisch, und wir haben nach der Entstehungs-geschichte dieses Werks keinen Grund, daran zu zweifeln.'

the Chinese Sages I shall think especially of Confucius and Mencius and Mo-tzŭ.[1] In each of these I think there was some truly prophetic quality which makes comparison with the Hebrew figures profitable.[2] Of the author of the *Tao Tê Ching*,[3] traditionally called Lao-tzŭ,[4] and of the Taoist Chuang-tzŭ[5] I think

[1] Of Confucius and Mencius there are innumerable studies, but Mo-tzŭ is less known to western readers. For a brief account of him, with references to a number of works which deal with his teaching, cf. my *Submission in Suffering*, 1951, pp. 108 ff. For the fullest account of him in English cf. Y. P. Mei, *Motse, the neglected Rival of Confucius*, 1934, and *The Ethical and Political Works of Motse*, 1929, and in German, A. Forke, *Mê Ti, des Sozialethikers und seiner Schüler philosophische Werke*, 1922. Translations of substantial parts, or the whole, of the surviving texts may be seen in the works of Mei and Forke, and also in L. Tomkinson, *The Social Teachings of Meh Tse* (Transactions of the Asiatic Society of Japan, 2nd series, iv), 1927. Where passages are cited the rendering of Mei will normally be followed. For Confucius I shall rely mainly, though not exclusively, on the *Analects*. On these R. Wilhelm (*Confucius and Confucianism*, E.Tr. by G. H. and A. P. Danton, 1931, p. 134) observes: 'All in all, we have before us in this collection solid, reliable material, which must always be taken into primary consideration in any presentation of the doctrines of Confucius.' For Mencius I shall rely on the classic that bears his name. On this Wilhelm (*ibid.*, p. 139) says: 'This book is in excellent textual condition and may be regarded as a perfect reproduction of the teachings of Mencius.'

[2] Liang Ch'i-ch'ao (*History of Chinese Political Thought*, 1930, p. 28) observes that 'all the great thinkers of China lived during the three hundred years between 530 and 230 B.C., the Golden Age of Chinese philosophy'. In the present study we are concerned with a few of the figures of this period, but less as thinkers or philosophers than as prophets.

[3] Legge's translation of the *Tao Tê Ching* may be found in *Sacred Books of the East*, xxxix, 1891, pp. 47 ff. The same rendering together with the Chinese text may be found in *The Original Chinese Texts of the Confucian Analects . . . and the Works of Lao-tsze, with their Japanese translation and their English translations and notes* (n.d., Tokyo). The Chinese text and French translation may be found in L. Wieger, *Taoïsme*, ii, 1913, pp. 18 ff., and J. J. L. Duyvendak, *Tao Tö King: Le Livre de la Voie et de la Vertu*, 1953. Of the innumerable other renderings of this work it may suffice to mention A. Waley, *The Way and its Power*, 1934, reprinted 1942, Ch'u Ta Kao, *Tao Tê Ching*, 1937, R. Wilhelm, *Laotse: Tao Te King*, 1923, and J. J. L. Duyvendak, *Tao Te Ching: The Book of the Way and its Virtue*, 1954. (On the two books by Duyvendak mentioned in this note cf. D. Bodde, *J.A.O.S.*, lxxiv, 1954, pp. 211 ff.)

[4] Many modern writers dispute the traditional view that Lao-tzŭ, an older contemporary of Confucius, composed the *Tao Tê Ching*, and not a few doubt whether he lived at all. For references to a number of these cf. *Submission in Suffering*, pp. 108 f.n. This question is of no moment to us here.

[5] On Chuang-tzŭ cf. E. R. Hughes, *Chinese Philosophy in Classical Times*, 1942,

it is harder to sustain the thesis that they deserve the name of prophet. Of others I shall make but occasional mention. My purpose is not to give an outline of Chinese thought and teaching on the themes dealt with by the Hebrew prophets, or themes which are common to the two groups, but to bring together dynamic figures in the two civilizations deserving of the name of prophet, and to set some aspects of their work side by side.

It has been said that the prophets of Israel were sometimes consulted by those who sought their services. Much more could have been said along these lines. But more characteristic of prophecy is the utterance that arises from an inner initiative, and that the prophet himself declares without any human request. When Amos went to the sanctuary of Bethel and uttered a word which alarmed the priest by its dangerous character,[1] he was not responding to an invitation. 'The lion hath roared, who will not fear; the Lord God hath spoken, who can but prophesy?' he asked.[2] He prophesied because he had to, and not because men consulted him. With far more poignancy Jeremiah tells how he was driven to prophesy against his own will. Though he vowed that he would prophesy no more he found a fire burning in his bones that would not be quenched, and he was forced into utterance.[3] In the case of the Chinese teachers, we find that many of their most penetrating sayings are uttered in response to some question. Much of the teaching of Mencius is developed in dialogue with various persons, rather than in the public addresses which the Hebrew prophets seem to have given. Similarly Confucius in his talks with his disciples by question and answer often draws them out and then gives his own utterance after they have spoken, or replies to their questions. Here we have a formal difference, but no more than a formal difference, between the Chinese and the Hebrew teachers. They belong to different societies, with different traditions. But

pp. 165 ff. Hughes observes that there can be little doubt that more than half of the thirty-three chapters of the book that bears his name were written by men who doubtless counted as his followers, but whose minds moved on a different plane from his (p. 165).

[1] Amos vii. 10 ff.   [2] Amos iii. 8.   [3] Jer. xx. 9.

Chinese and Hebrews alike feel themselves to be charged with a word of importance for the whole society in which they are set. In the more democratic Israelite society, the prophets spoke to the people at large on occasions, whereas in the non-democratic Chinese society the sages addressed themselves to the influential classes, as opportunity offered. But sages no less than prophets wished their influence to permeate the whole of society, and felt themselves to be charged with a mission to their world.

A further formal difference between the two groups of teachers may be found in the fact that whereas the Hebrew prophets often uttered their teaching in the shrines, the Chinese did not. Amos prophesied in the sanctuary of Bethel,[1] and Jeremiah in the Jerusalem Temple.[2] On another occasion we read that Jeremiah sent Baruch into the Temple to read out in the public hearing the oracles which he had written down at the prophet's dictation.[3] The fact that the Chinese teachers did not similarly proclaim their words in the shrines of China is of no profound significance, however, so far as prophetic quality is concerned. It is due to the fact that to Confucius the shrine was a place of sacrifice, and not a place of public address, whereas in Israel the shrine was both. I have already said that to understand men it is necessary to try to set ourselves in their times and judge them in relation to their own world, and not to a different one which they could not know. A prophet is a prophet, not because he is psychologically abnormal, or because he preaches in a shrine, but because he is charged with a word of God and passes that word on by such means as are open to him in the society in which he lives.

The prophets of Israel sometimes spoke in shrines. But they were not confined to the shrines. Nathan's rebuke of David[4] and Elijah's of Ahab[5] do not appear to have been spoken in a shrine. Prophets could exercise their ministry in their own homes,[6] or by the wayside,[7] or in the court,[8] as well as in the shrines. While

[1] Amos vii. 10 ff.   [2] Jer. vii. 2, xxvi. 2.   [3] Jer. xxxvi. 6.
[4] 2 Sam. xii. 1 ff.   [5] 1 Kings xxi. 17 ff.   [6] Cf. 2 Kings v. 9.
[7] Cf. 1 Kings xx. 38.
[8] Cf. 2 Sam. xxiv. 11, which indicates that Gad was attached to the court in an official capacity.

their activity in the shrines is not paralleled in the activity of the
Chinese teachers, every other form may be. Their teaching was not
limited to this place or that. It could be given in the hearing of
princes,[1] and it could equally be given in their homes[2] or elsewhere.[3] It is in the substance and the source of their message that
they may be most appropriately compared.

In the Old Testament we often read of schools of prophets.[4]
They lived together sometimes, and sometimes they functioned as
a group. The prophets whom Saul met after being anointed by
Samuel at Ramah were seized by a common and contagious
spirit of ecstasy.[5] The four hundred prophets whom Zedekiah
the son of Chenaanah led[6] were doubtless prophesying together in
a way that must have seemed profoundly impressive to all who
beheld. The lone Micaiah must have been at an enormous psychological disadvantage. There is no reason whatever to suppose that
all prophets belonged to such groups, though it is interesting to
observe that one story declares that Samuel once found himself
with such a group,[7] and Elisha is depicted as in such a group
at one time.[8] Of the nature of the groups we have little knowledge,
but presumably they each had a single head, as Zedekiah was the
head of the company in Ahab's time. That the greater prophets
had groups of followers is very probable, though we have but
little evidence of this. Amos does not give us the impression of
being the leader of a company when he prophesied at Bethel, but
there is no reason to suppose that all his utterances were made
there, or that all who listened to him were uninfluenced to attach

---

[1] Cf. *Analects* II, xix, III, xx, XIII, xv, xvi and elsewhere, *Mencius* I Part I, i. 1
and often. In the time of Mencius the title duke had been replaced by king, which
the heads of the states now arrogated to themselves.

[2] Cf. *Analects* VII, xxxiv, IX, xi.

[3] Cf. *Analects* IX, v. Of many of the sayings of Confucius we are given no
indication where they were uttered.

[4] Cf. 1 Sam. x. 5, 10, xix. 18 ff., 2 Kings ii. 3, 5, iv. 38. On these prophetic
guilds cf. M. A. van Oudenrijn, *Biblica*, vi, 1925, pp. 165 ff., where it is noted that
the term 'sons of the prophets' is only attested for the period 850–750 B.C., and
only for the northern Kingdom.

[5] 1 Sam. x. 5 f.   [6] 1 Kings xxii. 11 f.

[7] 1 Sam. xix. 20.   [8] 2 Kings iv. 38.

themselves to him. Jeremiah assuredly had one disciple in Baruch.[1]
In Isaiah we find a reference to 'my disciples',[2] and Wade suggests
that it was probably to these that Isaiah addressed most of his con-
solatory utterances.[3] It is improbable that there was any united
functioning of the great prophets and their disciples, comparable
with the examples that have been mentioned; but it is commonly
believed that they had their disciples who received of their teaching
and who treasured their utterances. We know that Jeremiah dic-
tated some of his oracles to Baruch;[4] but Baruch's roll cannot be
identified with the present book of Jeremiah. It is more probable
that the book of Jeremiah was compiled long after his death from
material preserved in various sources.[5] The Scandinavian school
stresses the importance of oral tradition, and believes that the
materials of the prophetic books were carried down in oral tradition for a long time before they were written down.[6] It is unnecessary to exclude written traditions, coming even from the prophet's own time,[7] as the roll of Baruch came from Jeremiah's time;
it is equally unnecessary to deny that oral transmission may also
have preserved many sayings that were first written down after
the prophet's death. But this presupposes circles of disciples where
the sayings were treasured. Mowinckel has attached great
importance to the circle of Isaiah's disciples,[8] and Kissane has
supposed that they continued to exist for a hundred and fifty

[1] Jer. xxxvi. 4 ff.
[2] Isa. viii. 16.
[3] *The Book of the Prophet Isaiah*, 1911, p. 59.
[4] Jer. xxxvi. 4, 32.
[5] Cf. S. Mowinckel, *Zur Komposition des Buches Jeremia*, 1914, and *Prophecy
and Tradition*, 1946, pp. 21 ff., 61 ff.; O Eissfeldt, *Einleitung in das Alte Testament*,
1934, pp. 161 ff.; Oesterley and Robinson, *Introduction to the Books of the Old
Testament*, 1934, pp. 224 ff.
[6] Cf. I. Engnell, *Gamla Testamentet*, i, 1945. The second volume of this work has
not appeared, and the promised English translation is not yet available. For a short
account in English of the approach of this school cf. E. Nielsen, *Oral Tradition*,
1954, in which there is a discussion of Jeremiah xxxvi.
[7] Cf. S. Mowinckel, *Prophecy and Tradition*, 1946, and G. Widengren, *Literary
and Psychological Aspects of the Hebrew Prophets*, 1948.
[8] Cf. *Jesaja-disiplene*, 1926.

years after his time.[1] There is thus a wide consensus of opinion which believes that the great prophets had followers, whether few or many, who were under their influence in more than a casual way, and who not merely heard the relatively few utterances that have been preserved, but who knew in a fuller way the power of the personality of the prophet, and who understood the message which he sought to deliver.

Of the Chinese Sages we have more certain knowledge that they had circles of disciples who were under their continuous influence and instruction. Confucius is said to have had more than seventy disciples.[2] A few figure again and again in the traditions, and especially the favourite Yen Hui, whose early death so deeply affected the Master.[3] The *Analects* were not compiled until after the death of Confucius, and may well have been preserved orally for a time. His disciples continued his work after his death and developed into various groups along different lines, stressing different aspects of the Master's teaching. E. R. Hughes observes that 'we can only distinguish three varieties of tradition with any accuracy'.[4] One of these is the philosophical line, in which the grandson of Confucius, Tzŭ Ssŭ, is the outstanding figure.[5] To

[1] Cf. *The Book of Isaiah*, ii, 1943, pp. lix ff., where it is held that Deutero-Isaiah was composed in the period of the exile on the basis of teaching which had been orally transmitted from the eighth-century prophet.

[2] He is credited with a total of 3,000 disciples, a figure which A. Forke (*Geschichte der alten chinesischen Philosophie*, p. 101) does not think unreasonably high. On the other hand, E. D. Edwards (*Confucius*, 1940, p. 64) thinks the figure is exaggerated. In the stricter sense his disciples are variously given as seventy-seven and seventy-two (cf. Forke, *loc. cit.*). Legge (*The Chinese Classics*, i, 2nd ed., pp. 112 ff.) lists the names of eighty-six followers whose names have come down to us. E. R. Hughes (*Chinese Philosophy in Classical Times*, p. 68) says more or less reliable information about some twenty of them is known. A. Waley (*The Analects of Confucius*, p. 19) says far fewer than this ever appear as definite 'frequenters of his gate'.   [3] Cf. *Analects* XI, vi, viii.

[4] *Op. cit.*, p. 68. *Han-Fei-tzŭ* mentions eight Confucian schools. Cf. *Works*, chapter l. This passage is not included in W. K. Liao's translation (*The Complete Works of Han Fei Tzŭ*, i, 1939), which goes only as far as chapter xxx. The Chinese text of the passage here referred to is cited in Forke, *Mê Ti*, p. 75.

[5] On Tzŭ Ssŭ cf. Hughes, *op. cit.*, pp. 31 f.; Forke, *Geschichte der alten chinesischen Philosophie*, pp. 158 ff.; L. Wieger, *Histoire des Croyances religieuses et des opinions philosophiques en Chine*, 1922, pp. 221 f. (this work appeared in English, translated by E. C. Werner, in 1927).

him the compilation of the *Doctrine of the Mean* is traditionally ascribed, and there seems good reason to believe that there is substance in this, even though the work may have been added to later.[1]

Mencius is said to have been a disciple of Tzŭ Ssŭ's school,[2] and that he himself had disciples is clear from the book which bears his name. According to tradition it was compiled by Mencius himself in old age with the help of a disciple,[3] and it presents us with a teacher who often developed his message in discussion with his followers, as Confucius himself had done.

Mo-tzŭ again not only had followers, but organized them with a view to the continuation of his work under a leader who has been likened to the Pope.[4] We know that they broke up into rival groups under three different leaders, each claiming that the true authority was vested in him alone.[5]

All of this sufficiently indicates that these Chinese teachers thought that the message which was entrusted to them was of enduring moment to men. Though their word was born out of their own times it did not belong wholly to their own times. There was a timeless quality about it, because fundamental principles which could be applied and reapplied to other times ran through it all. For it was not born wholly out of their times. It was a divine message. Confucius could say 'Heaven produced the virtue that is in me',[6] and could use words which implied his con-

[1] Cf. Hughes, *op. cit.*, p. 32. Hughes discusses this question more fully in *The Great Learning and the Mean-in-Action*, pp. 86 ff.

[2] Cf. Forke, *op. cit.*, p. 191.

[3] Cf. E. R. Hughes, *Chinese Philosophy in Classical Times*, p. 96.

[4] The title of this office was Chü-tzŭ and within thirty years of the death of Mo-tzŭ he had been succeeded by three holders of this office. In *Mo-tzŭ* l, we have a reference to three hundred disciples of Mo-tzŭ's who were manning the walls of Sung, and in the *Lü Shih Ch'un Ch'iu* XIX, iii, there is a reference to the heroic sacrifice of Mo-tzŭ's successor as Chü-tzŭ, together with a large band of disciples. The number is variously given as eighty-three and one hundred and eighty-three by different writers. The Chinese text to which I have had access has the latter number. So R. Wilhelm's German Tr., *Frühling und Herbst des Lü Bu We*, 1928, pp. 327 f.

[5] Cf. *Han-Fei-tzŭ*, *loc. cit.*, and *Chuang-tzŭ* xxxiii. 2.

[6] *Analects* VII, xxii.

viction that he was immortal till his work was done.[1] Mencius was not a rival teacher, but a follower of Confucius, with a particular interest in the political side of his teaching, and he sought to bring out and to apply to the problems of his own day the principles which he found in the Master's teaching. Mo-tzŭ, again, passionately believed that there was entrusted to him by God a message that was urgently and profoundly needed by the world. Here is something comparable with the moral earnestness of the Hebrew prophets. These men were the spokesmen of God. Their message did not come by the suspension of their personality, as the Hebrew prophet's message is thought by some to have come, and they did not disdain the use of the mind which God had given to them. But they acknowledged that they were raised up to do their work, and that they were the spokesmen of the Unseen. Despite all that differentiates them from the prophets of Israel, therefore, they may fairly be treated as prophetic figures and placed alongside the Hebrew figures, and a few aspects of the teaching of both groups may be set side by side. It will be my aim to be as objective as possible, not exaggerating differences to put the Chinese teachers at a disadvantage as against the more familiar Old Testament prophets, but not disguising differences where differences exist.

[1] *Analects* IX, v. 3.

II

The Prophet as Statesman

ODERN writers frequently refer to the prophets of Israel as statesmen. It is probable that they would have repudiated any such description of themselves, and it is certainly far from adequate. Nevertheless, it is true that they were deeply interested in the affairs of state and constantly dealt with such matters in their oracles.

At the time of the establishment of the monarchy, when the prophets first come prominently before us as an order, we find them stirring up the national sentiment against the Philistines.[1] They were not only devotees of the national God, but also eager patriots who sought to free the nation from a foreign yoke. The relation of Samuel to these groups is not clear, but he was certainly in touch with them and shared their interests. For it was he who anointed Saul privately, and commissioned him to lead Israel in a bid for freedom.[2] In the earliest account of the founding of the monarchy, the appointment of a king is ascribed to the divine initiative operating through Samuel, and it is stated that it sprang from the divine compassion for Israel under the Philistine heel.[3] In another story, which is less creditable to Samuel, he incites Saul into a war of wanton aggression against the Amalekites in revenge for things that had happened centuries before.[4] Later we find Nathan, an authentic prophet who had not hesitated to rebuke

---

[1] Cf. 1 Sam. x. 5. We are not told here what was the content of the prophesying, but it is significant that it took place in the neighbourhood of the evidence of the Philistine control, and the setting of the story would suggest that these prophets, like Samuel, were concerned for the subject condition of Israel.

[2] 1 Sam. x. 1, 7. Again it is from the context that we learn that the purpose of this anointing was deliverance from the Philistines, who are not actually mentioned here.

[3] 1 Sam. ix. 16.

[4] 1 Sam. xv. 2 f.

David for his adultery with Bathsheba,[1] taking a hand in the succession intrigues that attended David's senility, and helping to put Solomon on the throne instead of his elder brother, Adonijah.[2] During the reign of Solomon Ahijah the prophet encouraged Jeroboam to head a revolt,[3] and though this was for the moment nipped in the bud and Jeroboam had to take refuge abroad in Egypt,[4] at Solomon's death he returned to lead the northern tribes in splitting the unity of the kingdom.[5] When Rehoboam planned to reduce the northern tribes to submission, it was another prophet, Shemaiah by name, who effectively checked him by condemning his purpose.[6] Later we find prophets continually taking a hand in the revolutions that marked the history of the northern kingdom.[7] The most familiar and the most outstanding instance of this is the story of the overthrow of the house of Omri. The prophets Elijah and Elisha successively led the opposition to that house, and when Jehu led the revolution it was at the instigation of a prophet sent to him by Elisha.[8] We even find that revolution in the neighbouring kingdom of Damascus was fostered by a prophet.[9] All of this abundantly illustrates the political, and usually revolutionary, interest of many of the earlier prophets.

That there were other prophets who were not revolutionary is probable enough, and certain for the time of Ahab. For here we read of large numbers of prophets attached to the court and subservient to the king, ready to give him in the name of God the advice that reflected his own wishes.[10] They were ready to stir up king and people against foreign foes and to promise the help of the God of Israel, and superficially they were doing exactly what Samuel had done at the time of the establishment of the monarchy. But Micaiah was the forerunner of a succession of prophets who had a profounder idea of patriotism,[11] and who tested policies by their wisdom and not merely by whether they chimed with the mood of the moment and reflected a blind belief that God was tied to Israel, and was bound to help them against the foreigner.

[1] 2 Sam. xii. 1 ff. [2] 1 Kings i. 11 ff. [3] 1 Kings xi. 29 ff.
[4] 1 Kings xi. 40. [5] 1 Kings xii. 2 f. [6] 1 Kings xii. 22 ff.
[7] Cf. 1 Kings xiv. 14, xv. 29, xvi. 1 ff., 12. [8] 2 Kings ix. 1 ff.
[9] 2 Kings viii. 7 ff. [10] 1 Kings xxii. 6 ff. [11] 1 Kings xxii. 8 ff.

When we come to the prophets of the eighth and following centuries, we no longer find them stirring up revolution. Yet their interest in political conditions is abundantly clear. Many of their contemporaries were like those earlier prophets, ready to promise divine help against any foreign foe. In the days of Samuel it might well have been that the religion of Israel would have perished but for the political freedom which the monarchy brought. The popular prophets of the eighth century could well have claimed that an even greater danger threatened that religion now. For Assyria was expanding its power and becoming an increasing menace in the west, and the policy of Assyria was to impose the worship of its gods upon conquered people. Yet in that age Amos and Hosea could hold before men the power of Assyria as God's means of disciplining His people,[1] and Isaiah could speak of God summoning Assyria to do His work.[2] To these prophets patriotism was not to be measured by hatred of the enemy, though there is no evidence that any of these had anything but hatred of Assyria.[3] Isaiah, who spoke of Assyria as the rod of Yahweh's anger to chastise His people,[4] could also speak of the contempt with which Assyria would be cast aside when she had served His purpose, and of the punishment that would be meted out to her because her acts, though they could be used to serve the purpose of God, were born of nothing higher than the cruel will of her own heart.[5]

These eighth-century prophets and their successors were, however, deeply interested in political affairs and in the principles of sound government. And because in that age Israel was continually being drawn into the maelstrom of the struggle for power between Assyria and Egypt, that caught all the small states of Syria and Palestine and involved them in its turmoil, it was frequently

[1] Amos does not mention Assyria by name, but Amos v. 27 would clearly suggest to his contemporaries Assyria as the power whereby the sorrows he predicted would be brought on Israel. Hosea more openly stated that Assyria would be the instrument of the divine discipline; cf. Hos. xi. 5.

[2] Cf. Isa. vii. 18 f., 20.

[3] Cf. what I have written in *The Relevance of Apocalyptic*, 2nd ed., 1947, p. 19.

[4] Isa. x. 5.   [5] Isa. x. 12 ff.

of international affairs that they spoke. At the time of the Syro
Ephraimitish war Isaiah could approach the king with his advice,
and years later he could rebuke Hezekiah for his negotiations with
the messengers of Merodach-baladan.[2] He could publicly de
nounce the intrigues with Egypt in preparation for the event
which led to the fall of Ashdod in 711 B.C.,[3] and had no confidenc
in the revolt against Sennacherib.[4] Yet when the situation wa
desperate the king sent for him to consult him, and Isaiah now
counselled calm resistance and promised the deliverance of Jeru
salem[5] whose safety he had consistently announced.[6]

Throughout his career Jeremiah predicted calamity at the hand
of foreign foes. At the outset of his career it seems to have been th
Scythian peril that provided the background of his warnings
though some scholars doubt if there was any Scythian peril at all.
Later, it was certainly the Babylonian advance, and again near th
end of his known ministry it was the approach of Nebucha
drezzar to crush the revolt into which Zedekiah was drawn which
constituted the peril of which he spoke—a peril which he un
waveringly declared to be of fatal moment for his people. Tha
he was held to be the enemy of his people is not surprising
Nebuchadrezzar appears to have heard of him and to have regarded
him as pro-Babylonian.[8] Yet though in time of war he weakened
the resistance of the state,[9] and to the Jerusalem and the Baby
lonian authorities alike he appeared to be pro-Babylonian,[10] thi
was to misunderstand the man and his message.

To Jeremiah, as to the prophets of the eighth and seventh

---

[1] Isa. vii. 1 ff.   [2] Isa. xxxix. 3 ff.
[3] Isa. xx.   [4] Cf. Isa. xxxi.
[5] Cf. Isa. xxxvii. 6 f., 21 ff.   [6] Cf. Isa. i. 8, iv. 5 f., xxxi. 5, xxxiii. 20 ff
[7] For the common view that the Scythian peril formed the background of
Jeremiah's early prophecies, cf. J. Skinner, *Prophecy and Religion*, 1922, pp. 35 ff.
and J. M. P. Smith, *The Prophets and their Times*, 2nd ed., revised by W. A. Irwin
1941, pp. 131 ff. This view is contested by F. Wilke, in *Alttestamentliche Studien*
(Kittel Festschrift), 1913, pp. 222 ff., J. Lewy, *Forschungen zur alten Geschicht*
Vorderasiens, 1925, pp. 51 ff., P. Volz, *Der Prophet Jeremia*, 1922, pp. 57 f., J. P
Hyatt, *J.B.L.*, lvi, 1937, pp. 193 ff., W. Rudolph, *Jeremia*, 1947, pp. 41 ff., W. A. L
Elmslie, *How Came our Faith*, 1948, p. 314 n.
[8] Cf. Jer. xxxix. 11 f.   [9] Jer. xxxviii. 4.   [10] Cf. Jer. xxxvii. 13

centuries that preceded him, all this political interest and activity arose from something deeper than an arm-chair interest in the affairs of their day. They were not merely men who sized up the situation better than others, in the sense that they better estimated the relative strength of Assyria and Egypt, or Babylonia and Egypt, and that they had a truer idea than others of the reliability of Egypt. It was not because they believed in the irresistible power of Assyria and of Babylon that they counselled men as they did. Let it be remembered that when all seemed lost Isaiah counselled calm resistance to Assyria and the defiant closing of the gates of Jerusalem against the armies of Sennacherib.[1] Moreover the prophet who could speak of Yahweh summoning Assyria to do His work and then casting her aside afterwards clearly had no belief in the irresistible might of Assyria. All the prophets were sure that God was in final control of human affairs. They did not suppose that all human history reflected His will, and they certainly did not release men and nations from the responsibility for their own acts. Yet they were sure that when God chose to protect His people all human forces were powerless against Him. If, then, they were sure that He would not restrain Assyria and Babylon from bringing devastation and ruin upon Israel it was not because He could not, or because of the vast material forces of these powers. Their political counsels were therefore based on religious principles, and those religious principles at bottom had nothing whatever to do with Assyria and Babylon, but only with Israel and her relation to God.[2] They were sure that Israel was not walking in the way of obedience to God's will, and was not, therefore, sensitive to His guidance. In the internal life of the nation they saw moral and social disorders which they perceived to spring from religious disloyalty. All these disorders were to them symptoms of disease in the life of the people, but the disease itself lay deeper, in the very spirit of the nation. From that

[1] 2 Kings xix. 32 ff. Cf. Isa. xxx. 15.
[2] Cf. R. B. Y. Scott, *The Relevance of the Prophets,* 1944, p. 172: 'The social evils which the prophets denounced were not political and economic merely; they were at the same time *religious* evils.'

spirit the external policies no less than the internal life of the nation arose, and the nation that was not sensitive to the guidance of God in its internal life could not be sensitive to that guidance in its external life. And without that guidance the prophets were certain that it could only stumble forward to disaster. They were not men who wanted the troubles they prophesied—and that was why it was quite wrong to regard Jeremiah as pro-Babylonian. They earnestly wanted their people to return to the way of wisdom and to bring their spirit and their life into accord with the will of God. They were sure that if they did this, God could deliver them from their present and future perils and could give them guidance in all their policies.

I have said that there were popular prophets whose patriotism was more narrowly based. There is every indication that Nahum was one of these.[1] At the time of the fall of Nineveh he fiercely hailed the destruction of the proud and oppressive power of Assyria, and in brilliant poetry expressed the glee with which the end of her empire was watched in Judah and the west. That was but natural, indeed, and there is no reason to suppose that Isaiah would not have shared that glee, had he lived to witness that day. He would have rejoiced to see all the vaunted might of Assyria swept away, and the vessel of God's anger now cast away as a potsherd. But whereas Isaiah had given wise counsel to men, the only word of Nahum's that has been preserved for us is one of exultation at the overthrow of the cruel oppressor. Still more directly does this contrast with the message of his contemporary Jeremiah.[2] Though he too lived at the time of the fall of Nineveh, no paean of rejoicing which he uttered has been preserved for us, but only warnings. For he rightly perceived that Judah would derive no benefit from the overthrow of Nineveh, but that her conqueror would take over the task of disciplining Israel as God's

[1] Cf. T. H. Robinson, *Prophecy and the Prophets in Ancient Israel*, 1923, p. 114: 'Nahum is a representative of that purely patriotic type of prophecy which has left little trace elsewhere in our Old Testament.'

[2] Cf. J. M. P. Smith, *The Prophets and their Times*, 2nd ed., pp. 152 f.: 'Nothing could be more striking than the contrast between Nahum and Jeremiah in their attitudes toward the fall of Nineveh.'

instrument. The event proved that he was a more penetrating statesman. For ere long Jerusalem suffered at the hand of Nebuchadrezzar as she had never suffered at the hand of the Assyrian.

When it came to the turn of Babylon to fall, the unknown author of Isaiah xiii[1] hailed that fall with a relish that is reminiscent of Nahum's at the time of the fall of Nineveh. His contemporary Deutero-Isaiah also shared that relish,[2] but like Isaiah and Jeremiah he delivered a much fuller message than this. He watched the rise of Cyrus and stirred the hopes of his people that the Persian prince would overthrow the Babylonian empire and restore the Jews to their own land.[3] But this was the basis of a powerful call to them to utter loyalty to God and to the realization that if He had chosen them to be His people it was that through them He might claim all men for Himself.[4] The divine election and the divine redemption laid an obligation on her which could only be discharged in her mission to the world. The political interest of Deutero-Isaiah was quite different from that of the pre-exilic prophets, because he lived in a different age. Since the prophet spoke primarily to his own generation it was inevitable that the message was determined in part by the conditions of his age, even though there was also a timeless element in it. Deutero-Isaiah spoke not of judgement on his people, but of deliverance for them. Hence he did not derive his message from a diagnosis of the spiritual condition of his people, as reflected in the moral and social conditions that prevailed amongst them. He could speak in terms of rebuke, indeed, and lamented that they were blind and deaf to the significance of the great hour which was upon them,[5] and that they did not greet the deliverance with a mood that matched the greatness of the hour. But his word was one of salvation and deliverance rather than of judgement. Nevertheless, he pressed upon them the corollary of the deliverance in the

---

[1] E. J. Kissane, *The Book of Isaiah*, i, 1941, p. 155, thinks that Isa. xiii. 1–xiv. 2 was originally an oracle spoken by Isaiah against Assyria, which was later modified and made to refer to Babylon. Most scholars, however, believe that it was written in the sixth century B.C., at some time before the fall of Babylon.

[2] Cf. Isa. xlvii.   [3] Cf. Isa. xliv. 28, xlv. 1 ff.

[4] Cf. Isa. xlii. 6 f.   [5] Isa. xlii. 18 ff.

loyalty it demanded of them. The salvation from the external oppressor was to him a new divine initiative in grace, which must have consequences in the whole life of the people if it was not to fail in its purpose. To him no less than to the pre-exilic prophets the life of the people was one, and the external relations and the internal life must be closely bound together. To them the symptom of the lack of health of the people was to be seen in the inner conditions of society; to him the evidence of health must be found in the loyalty by which it would be expressed—a loyalty which must show itself not alone in social conditions within, but in the acceptance of her mission without.

All of this and a great deal more that might be added will demonstrate the interest of the greater prophets, as well as of their predecessors, in the political conditions of their times. They did not hold office in the state, but they continually intervened in the affairs of the state. Sometimes they were consulted by kings, as Isaiah was by Hezekiah[1] and Jeremiah by Zedekiah,[2] and sometimes they approached kings, as Isaiah approached Ahaz.[3] In either case, when they stood before kings they did not hesitate to give frank advice, and while there were always prophets to offer palatable advice, the greater prophets were completely independent and courageous, and more often than not offered unwelcome advice. But they did not limit their activity to king or court. They spoke in shrines, as Amos did at Bethel[4] or Jeremiah in Jerusalem,[5] where their word would be heard by the common people, and without fear or favour they warned the people no less than their rulers. For Israel was always an essentially democratic people. While it knew nothing of the modern forms of democratic government, and its democracy was quite differently organized from that of ancient Greece or Rome, it was nevertheless democratic. For democracy is to be seen more in the spirit than in the forms. The modern world has seen tyrannies function-

---

[1] Cf. Isa. xxxvii. 2 ff.   [2] Cf. Jer. xxxvii. 17 ff., xxxviii. 14 ff.
[3] Cf. Isa. vii. 3 ff.   [4] Cf. Amos vii. 10 ff.
[5] Cf. Jer. vii. 2 ff., xxvi. 2 ff. Cf. also Jer. xxxvi. 6 ff., where Baruch is sent to read the roll of Jeremiah's prophecies in the Temple.

ing through the machinery of popular election, in which a single party is allowed to have candidates, and the people vote like sheep. Without popular elections and parliamentary government Israel knew more of the spirit of democracy. There was normally —save in periods such as Ahab's reign and Manasseh's reign— freedom to discuss the affairs of the state, and to influence public opinion by open advocacy, and not alone by underground methods. In all states except the ruthless police state, governments are influenced by public opinion, which may develop in a variety of ways. In no state is openly revolutionary activity tolerated, and it was but natural, therefore, that when prophets instigated revolution they did it secretly. But if one of the hall-marks of true democracy is freedom to discuss the policies of the state and to seek to mould public opinion, then the prophets of Israel are the evidence that by and large Israel had that mark. It is true that Jeremiah was imprisoned and suffered grievously,[1] but it must be remembered that this was in time of war, and that he appeared to friend and foe to be pro-Babylonian, and that the most democratic of modern states would give short shrift in war time to one who preached desertion to the enemy as Jeremiah did.[2] It is also true that there were periods when liberty was limited, and many prophets may have suffered for their boldness.[3] Of two only do we have direct record that they were put to death,[4] and one of them was killed by the hard and headstrong Jehoiakim, who feared neither God nor man, and who defiantly burned the roll of Jeremiah's prophecies despite the appeal of his courtiers.[5] Yet even though there were times when kings sought to silence criticism, the bold willingness of the prophets to brave their displeasure carried the claim that in Israel there were rights which were not granted by king or state, but which rested on the will of God.

In many respects the Sages of China stand in marked contrast to the prophets of Israel. They did not harangue the people in temple and mart, but wherever they could find hearers, whether

---

[1] Cf. Jer. xxxvii. 15, 20, xxxviii. 6.   [2] Cf. Jer. xxi. 9.
[3] Cf. 1 Kings xviii. 4, xix. 10, 2 Kings xxi. 16.
[4] Cf. Jer. xxvi. 23, 2 Chron. xxiv. 20 f.   [5] Cf. Jer. xxxvi. 23 ff.

amongst their disciples or amongst others, they were ready to speak on the policies of states. They were profoundly interested in the principles of sound government, not as an academic exercise, but in the concrete setting of the affairs of their own time.

Unlike the prophets of Israel, Confucius aspired to office in the state. He is said to have claimed that if any prince employed him, within twelve months he could effect notable reforms and within three years he could perfect the government.[1] For a time he was employed as a minister,[2] and he is said to have carried through such reforms that neighbouring princes were alarmed and sought to counter his influence.[3] When they sent eighty beautiful singing girls to beguile the prince, and the Sage was left for three days without audience, he renounced his office,[4] though he withdrew from the court with manifest reluctance, hoping against hope that he might be recalled.[5] For though Confucius longed for office, he was not prepared to accept it on conditions which impaired his dignity or curtailed his power. This story is told by Ssŭ-ma Ch'ien,[6] and there is a brief reference to it in the *Analects*, where it is said that the people of Ch'i sent a present of singing girls, as the result of which no court was held for three days, in consequence of which Confucius took his departure.[7] But Professor Dubs rejects the whole story as a fabrication or midrash, and attributes the Sage's loss of office to a great diplomatic victory which he achieved, and which caused such irritation to the prince

---

[1] *Analects* XIII, x.

[2] A. Waley, *The Analects of Confucius*, p. 14, says: 'There is not the slightest indication that he ever obtained such a position.' Other scholars find no reason to doubt the tradition. So Forke, *Geschichte der alten chinesischen Philosophie*, pp. 103 f.

[3] Cf. Legge, *The Chinese Classics*, i, 2nd ed., pp. 71 ff. For an account of the phenomenal reforms which Confucius is said to have effected in the office of magistrate of Chung-tu, cf. *Chia Yü* I, 1a, Sect. i, § 1 (R. P. Kramers, *K'ung Tzŭ Chia Yü*, 1950, pp. 201 f.), and Ssŭ-ma Ch'ien, *Shih Chi* xlvii (E. Chavannes, *Les Mémoires historiques de Se-ma Ts'ien*, v, 1905, p. 327, or R. Wilhelm, *Confucius and Confucianism*, E.Tr. by G. H. and A. P. Danton, 1931, p. 23).

[4] Cf. Legge, *loc. cit.*, p. 75.

[5] Cf. Legge, *ibid.*, p. 76. A reference to the reluctance with which Confucius withdrew may perhaps stand in *Mencius* V Part 2, i. 4.

[6] *Shih Chi* xlvii (Chavannes, *op. cit.*, v, pp. 327 ff., or Wilhelm, *op. cit.*, pp. 23 ff.).

[7] *Analects* XVIII, iv.

he served that Confucius feared his life might be in danger, and he accordingly took advantage of a minor slight and left without resigning.[1] Whatever the cause he renounced his office and took his departure from the state of Lu.

When he was asked whether it was right to hoard a jewel or to sell it, he replied that he would sell it, provided he secured a proper price.[2] In the mind of both questioner and Sage it was clear that the point of the question was the suggestion that Confucius ought to take office in the public interest.[3] But he was as uncompromising as any of the Hebrew prophets where his fundamental principles were concerned, and to be in office when his advice was not followed and he was not supported by the conduct of the prince was intolerable to him. He was not even prepared to accept a gift from one who had sought his advice but had not followed it.[4] All this was not born simply of the stiff propriety which always marked Confucius, but was effective loyalty to his own principles. He was no mere hireling, but one who sought to rectify the government, and one of his most cherished ideas was that rectification began at the top. He had an exaggerated idea of the power of example,[5] but he was probably right in supposing that when he was neglected by the prince who employed him his own influence would be diminished. In truth Confucius was a statesman as much, or as little, as the prophets of Israel. He was essentially a prophet, and the place for the prophet is not in office, but rather as the mentor of the state. The successful statesman has need of integrity of character and strength of purpose, but he must be more ready to compromise than the prophet by his very nature can.[6]

Whenever Confucius had access to princes he spoke with a

[1] Cf. *J.A.O.S.*, lxvi, 1946, pp. 273 ff.
[2] *Analects* IX, xii.
[3] Cf. Legge's note in *The Chinese Classics*, i, 2nd ed., p. 221.
[4] Cf. Legge, *op. cit.*, i, p. 68. In this respect Mencius was less particular; cf. *Mencius* III Part 2, iv. On this cf. Legge, *The Chinese Classics*, ii, 2nd ed., pp. 53 ff.
[5] On this see below, pp. 67 f.
[6] E. D. Edwards (*Confucius*, 1940, p. 40) says: 'Unsuccessful both in public and in private life, he was keenly conscious of his failure but unwilling to admit it.'

frankness equal to that of the Hebrew prophets. Though he had little of their ruggedness, but was always the polished gentleman there was as much force in his rapier thrusts as there was in the bludgeon blows of the prophets of Israel. When the duke o Ch'i, who was overshadowed by his ministers and who wa planning to set his eldest son aside from succeeding him, asked Confucius about government, the Sage replied: 'Let the prince be prince and the minister be minister; let the father be father and the son be son.'[1] More blunt was his reply to another who asked how to get rid of thieves within his state: 'If you, Sir, were no covetous men would not steal, even though you paid them to do it.'[2] When asked about military tactics, he replied tartly that he understood all about sacrificial vessels, but not about military affairs, and to add point to his rebuke he took his departure the next day.[3] When a powerful officer of state asked the Sage the meaning of the saying 'It is better to pay court to the stove than to the south-west corner'—which may be paraphrased 'It is better

[1] *Analects* XII, xi. Cf. the note in Legge, *op. cit.*, i, p. 256 n., and in W. E Soothill, *The Analects of Confucius*, 1910, pp. 580, 582. Chavannes (*op. cit.*, v, pp 305 f.n.) objects to the view that there was any veiled thrust in this reply, on the ground that the Duke approved of the answer he received and that the interpretation does not tally with the chronology of the life of Confucius, as presented by Ssǔ-ma Ch'ien. The chronological difficulty seems the more serious, but other scholars accept the tradition. While some doubt must attach to it, it certainly gives a much greater significance to the Sage's reply than the vapid remark it otherwise becomes. Cf. also *Analects* XIII, iii, where the apparently innocent observation of Confucius that the first thing to do in government is to rectify names carried an implication that the unfilial prince of Wei, who had usurped his father's throne, ought to yield the throne to his father and so to behave as a son Cf. Legge's note, *The Chinese Classics*, i, 2nd ed., pp. 263 f., and L. Giles, *The Sayings of Confucius*, 1949 ed., p. 43 n. E. D. Edwards observes that 'Confucius's sayings were almost always coloured by the nature of the situation with which they were concerned, or of the person to whom they were addressed. If asked about administration, for instance, his reply was invariably directed to the weaknesses of the particular government which he knew to be in the mind of his questioner. It was this habit of going straight to the point that made him unpopular with the officials and rulers of the states he visited' (*Confucius*, 1940, pp. 46 f.).

[2] *Analects* XII, xviii. Waley finds here the suggestion 'that the ruler's moral force operates directly on the people, as a magic, not merely as an example' (*op. cit.*, p. 167 n.).

[3] *Analects* XV, i. 1.

:o be on good terms with the cook than with the gods'—Confucius repudiated the implied suggestion that it would pay him :o be on good terms with his questioner in the noble words 'He who offends against Heaven has none to whom he can pray.'[1] When two of his own disciples had taken service with one who was planning to usurp power, the would-be usurper asked Confucius if they would make great ministers. He replied that they were not more than ordinary. When further asked if their loyalty could be depended on, he replied that they would not be loyal to a parricide or a regicide, thus skilfully and indirectly, but none the less pointedly, expressing his own reproof.[2]

Confucius did not stir up revolution, as some of the earlier Hebrew prophets did, but he recognized that in certain circumstances revolution was justifiable. In the *Shu Ching* it is recognized that in some situations to take up arms against a ruler who has forfeited the throne by his conduct is not rebellion.[3] Confucius praised Wu Wang, the founder of the Chou dynasty, who executed his predecessor,[4] and later Mencius offered his justification of this act.[5] To Confucius, while government was of the people and not by the people, it was essentially for the people. When it was as it should be it would be accepted by the people without discussion, but when it was not as it should be discontents were inevitable. It was then the duty of ministers to remonstrate with the ruler,[6] and if unheeded to retire,[7] and revolution

---

[1] *Analects* III, xiii. Cf. the notes in Legge, *op. cit.*, i, 2nd ed., p. 159, and Soothill, *op. cit.*, pp. 197 f. Waley renders the concluding sentence: 'He who has put himself in the wrong with Heaven has no means of expiation left.'

[2] *Analects* XI, xxiii.

[3] Cf. *Shu Ching* IV Book 3, ii. 3 f. L. S. Hsü, *The Political Philosophy of Confucius*, 1932, p. 184, says: 'The Classics repeatedly declare that to take up arms against a tyrannical rule is not a rebellion but a deed carrying out the will of God.'

[4] *Analects* VIII, xx, XIX, xxii.

[5] *Mencius* I Part 2, viii.

[6] Cf. *Analects* XIV, xxiii, and *Li Chi* xv. 21. Translations of the *Li Chi* may be found in *Sacred Books of the East*, xxvii and xxviii, 1885 (by J. Legge), in S. Couvreur, *Li Ki*, 2 vols., 1913 (2nd ed.), 1899 (with Chinese text and Latin and French translations), and in R. Wilhelm, *Li Gi, das Buch der Sitte des älteren und üngeren Dai*, 1930 (German translation only).

[7] Cf. *Analects* XI, xxiii. 3. For this cf. also *Mencius* II Part 2, v. 5.

was not to be undertaken save as a last resort.¹ Reference has been made to usurpers and would-be usurpers whom Confucius condemned. But in these cases the conditions which could alone justify it were missing. Revolution that was born of personal ambition was no more acceptable to Confucius than to the Hebrew prophets. The mandate of Heaven was upon Wu,² just as the prophets declared that the mandate of God was upon those whom they stirred to acts of rebellion. It may be added that the Hebrew prophets were often quickly disillusioned about the rebels they encouraged, and the mandate was withdrawn.³

The times in which Confucius lived were very different from those of the Israelite prophets. In his time the central government of China had lost most of its authority, and the barons were more powerful than their lord. They continually warred amongst themselves and the people suffered inevitably.⁴ There was no external pressure here as in Israel, but an inner decay, which Confucius traced to a decay of the spirit. It is just here that he can be compared with the Hebrew prophets. His fundamental aim was to rectify men rather than policies, for he like them realized that the life of men and of states flows from the spirit, and that when that spirit is right the community will be healthy, contented and strong.

In this he was followed by Mencius, who had frequent access to rulers and governors, and whose interest in the principles of good government was often expressed with a boldness that well com-

---

¹ Cf. L. S. Hsü, *op. cit.*, p. 183: 'The Classics clearly suggest that a revolution by force should take place only as a last resort to improve political conditions and after all peaceful means have been tried out. The peaceful methods of making improvements consist of various forms of remonstrations with the ruler.'

² Cf. *Doctrine of the Mean* xviii. 3. Translations of the *Doctrine of the Mean* may be found in Legge, *The Chinese Classics*, i, 2nd ed., 1893; S. Couvreur, *Les Quatre Livres*, 1910; M. G. Pauthier, *Doctrine de Confucius*; L. A. Lyall and King Chien-Kün, *The Chung Yung*, 1927; E. R. Hughes, *The Great Learning and the Mean-in-Action*, 1942. Where passages are cited in the text, the rendering of Legge will normally be employed.

³ Cf. 1 Sam. xiii. 14, xv. 23 (Saul), 1 Kings xiv. 7 ff. (Jeroboam), 2 Kings x. 30 (Jehu).

⁴ Cf. Soothill, *The Analects of Confucius*, p. 21; L. S. Hsü, *op. cit.*, pp. 24 f.

pares with that of the Hebrew prophets.[1] Twice Mencius accepted office in the state of Ch'i,[2] but he fitted into such a position no more easily than Confucius. His independence of the ruler he served brought an element of constraint into their relations, and as Legge observes, 'where the two parties were so suspicious of each other, we need not wonder that they separated before long'.[3] Both Confucius and Mencius were persuaded that the government existed for the welfare of the people, and that its only stability rested on that welfare. It is unnecessary to multiply examples of this teaching. E. R. Hughes observes that politics was the master passion of Mencius,[4] and it is impossible to read the book that bears his name without finding examples of this interest, and without finding again and again the enunciation of his fundamental principle that the only successful government is good government, which studies the well-being of the people. When the state of Ch'i had attacked and conquered the state of Yen, and neighbouring states were forming an alliance to attack the victor, Mencius castigated the king of Ch'i by saying that if he had been content to deliver Yen from the misgovernment it had suffered and to consult the interests of the people, all would have been well; but he had given them oppressive and tyrannous government, so that he had merely succeeded in arousing the jealousy of his neighbours without adding to his own strength.[5] On another occasion, when speaking to the same ruler, Mencius bluntly declared that his efforts to increase his own power were as foolish as it would be to climb a tree to seek fish.[6] If only he would

[1] Legge observes: 'Never did Christian priest lift up his mitred front, or show his shaven crown, or wear his Geneva gown, more loftily in courts and palaces than Mencius, the Teacher, demeaned himself' (*The Chinese Classics*, ii, 2nd ed., p. 52). Cf. R. Wilhelm, who speaks of 'the great passion and the great courage with which Mencius entered the lists for the true and the good in the Confucian sense' (*Confucius and Confucianism*, E.Tr., p. 141).

[2] Cf. Legge, *op. cit.*, pp. 24 ff. References to Mencius's giving up office stand in *Mencius* II Part 2, x. 1 and VI Part 2, vi. 1.

[3] Cf. Legge, *op. cit.*, p. 27.

[4] *Chinese Philosophy in Classical Times*, p. 96.

[5] *Mencius* I Part 2, xi.

[6] *Mencius* I Part 1, vii. 16.

institute a benevolent government and seek the happiness of his people, their loyalty and affection would be so assured that he would be really great and strong. To one of the governors of this same state of Ch'i Mencius declared that his indifference to the sufferings of the people entrusted to his care in time of famine and misfortune was as criminal as that of a soldier who failed in his duty in the battle, and on finding that his words struck home to the conscience of the governor, Mencius reported the conversation to the king of the state and touched his conscience too.[1] Yet again, in conversation with the king of Ch'i, Mencius turned his selfish love of pleasure into a rebuke, and assured him that if he would study the happiness of his people as well as of himself, he would find in their devotion a source of irresistible strength.[2]

While this attaches greater weight to the conduct of the ruler than the Hebrew prophets would probably have attached, there is something of the same recognition that the life of the nation flowed from a single spring and that if the spring were purified the life would be rectified. They would have differed as to the location and the nature of the spring, since they did not attach the exaggerated importance to the influence of example which Confucius and his followers did. But they would have commended the candour of the rebuke to princes which had something of the savour of their own rebuke of both kings and the oppressive classes of society, while the benevolence desiderated by the Confucians had not a little in common with the *ḥesedh*[3] of the Hebrews.

As to the legitimacy of revolution, it is recorded that Mencius once observed to the king of Ch'i 'If the prince have great faults, they (i.e. the ministers) ought to remonstrate with him, and if he do not listen to them after they have done so again and again, they ought to dethrone him.'[4] It is little wonder that we read that

---

[1] *Mencius* II Part 2, iv.   [2] *Mencius* I Part 2, i. 8.

[3] This Hebrew word has been much discussed, and it defies translation by any one word in English. Cf. the monographs by N. Glueck, *Das Wort ḥesed im alttestamentlichen Sprachgebrauche*, 1927, and F. Asensio, *Misericordia et Veritas*, 1949. N. H. Snaith (*The Distinctive Ideas of the Old Testament*, 1944, pp. 94 ff.) calls it *covenant love*. See further below, p. 56

[4] *Mencius* V Part 2, ix. 1.

the king changed countenance. Mencius unmoved added: 'Let not your Majesty be offended. You asked me, and I dare not answer but according to truth.'

In the *Doctrine of the Mean*, which is attributed to the grandson of Confucius and the teacher of Mencius, but which is held to be in part a later expansion,[1] we find the self-cultivation of the ruler made the basis of good government.[2] This self-cultivation expresses itself in ever widening circles of benevolence until it reaches all the people. In the *Great Learning* self-cultivation is traced to the search for knowledge, leading to sincerity and the pure heart, and then to the rectification of the self which should express itself in the widening circles.[3] But here we find a doctrinaire treatment that has little of the prophetic quality of Confucius or Mencius.

In a later age Lord Shang held very different views, and taught that the business of the government was to govern, and that ruthless control was the basis of the only real stability.[4] For a time this was tried, but with results which were not encouraging, and I do not include Lord Shang amongst the prophetic figures of China. Confucius and Mencius are worthy to be placed alongside the prophets of the Old Testament, however. Their method and the form of their teaching stand in contrast to those of the Hebrews, but in spirit and in substance there is a greater affinity. They were not concerned to deal piecemeal with this ill or that, but wished to go down to the root. They recognized that political wisdom has a source which is deeper than politics, and with fearless courage they proclaimed their principles.

---

[1] Cf. E. R. Hughes, *The Great Learning and the Mean-in-Action*, 1942, pp. 86 ff.

[2] *Doctrine of the Mean* xx. 13.

[3] *Great Learning*, Text 4 f. Translations of the *Great Learning* may be found in Legge, *The Chinese Classics*, i, 2nd ed., 1893; Couvreur, *Les Quatre Livres*, 1910; M. G. Pauthier, *Doctrine de Confucius*; E. R. Hughes, *The Great Learning and the Mean-in-Action*. Where passages are quoted Legge's translation will be used.

[4] Cf. J. J. L. Duyvendak, *The Book of Lord Shang*, 1928, pp. 185 ff. On Shang Yang cf. A. Forke, *Geschichte der alten chinesischen Philosophie*, pp. 450 ff., L. Wieger, *Histoire des Croyances religieuses*, pp. 237 ff., and Duyvendak, *op. cit.*, pp. 41 ff., esp. pp. 75 ff.

Much closer to the Hebrew prophets stood Mo-tzŭ.[1] He, too, like Confucius and Mencius, is said to have held office for a short time in the state of Sung. The authority for this is a brief statement given by Ssŭ-ma Ch'ien in the *Shih Chi*.[2] This tradition is accepted by Fung Yu-lan,[3] but is disputed by some modern scholars.[4] If Mo-tzŭ did indeed hold office, his brief tenure seems to have ended in his being imprisoned by the master he served.[5] As always, the qualities which most become the prophet are other than those of the administrator, and the prophet in office is as uneasy as David in the armour of Saul.[6] In Mo-tzŭ's time the Emperor had but nominal authority and the various states were engaged in aggressive wars against one another, as they continued to be in the time of Mencius. The sufferings of the common people were intense, while luxury flaunted itself amongst the great, very much as in the times of some of the Old Testament prophets. Mo-tzŭ himself lived in simple conditions that were as austere as those of the prophet Elijah.[7]

[1] R. Wilhelm (*Die chinesischen Literatur*, 1926, p. 56) likens Mo-tzŭ to Savonarola.

[2] *Shih Chi*, end of Book lxxiv. The translation of Chavannes does not include this book. [3] *History of Chinese Philosophy*, i, 1937, p. 78.

[4] Cf. Williamson, *Mo Ti*, 1927, p. 3.

[5] Cf. Mei, *Motse the Neglected Rival of Confucius*, 1934, pp. 37, 45; Forke, *Mê Ti*, p. 30. [6] I Sam. xvii. 30 ff.

[7] Williamson, *op. cit.*, p. 3, says that 'he lived in a small house built of rough unworked timbers, with a thatched roof. He used none but earthenware utensils, and partook of the coarsest food. His clothing was of the simplest, of skin or grass according to the season.' The authority for this statement is stated to be Ssŭ-ma Ch'ien in the Preface to the *Shih Chi*. By this is probably meant Book cxxx of the *Shih Chi*, which is sometimes referred to as the Postface. I have been unable to find this reference, or to find mention of it in any other author. A section of Book cxxx of the *Shih Chi* was written by Ssŭ-ma T'an, the father of Ssŭ-ma Ch'ien (cf. Duyvendak, *The Book of Lord Shang*, p. 67, on the authorship and contents of this section), and in this section is a statement about Yao and Shun attributed to Mo-tzŭ by Ssŭ-ma T'an which is curiously like Williamson's statement about Mo-tzŭ himself. The passage is cited by Forke (*Mê Ti*, pp. 61 f.) and by Chavannes (*Les Mémoires historiques*, i, 1895, p. xiv), and it has some points of contact with what Mo-tzŭ says in *Mo-tzŭ* xxi (Mei, p. 122; Forke, p. 296; Tomkinson, pp. 74 f.). There can be little doubt that one who was so passionately sincere as Mo-tzŭ and who urged others to live by such austere standards himself shared them.

His concern with the wars of his time was as intimate as that of any of the Old Testament prophets, though the situation which he faced was very different from theirs. They belonged to a small state which was constantly becoming embroiled in the contests of its more powerful neighbours, and their message was addressed to their own people, though sometimes directed against those neighbours. The message of Mo-tzŭ was directed against the aggressors in the conflicts of his time and it was addressed with fearless courage to those aggressors.

Sometimes he denounced in general terms the aggression of the strong, and with prophetic fervour declared that while a petty thief was punished as a criminal the leader who annexed a city was treated as a hero.[1] Or again he protested that if the murderer of one man forfeited his life, the murderer of a hundred men forfeited it a hundredfold, and he who attacked a state yet more. To applaud this greatest criminal while punishing the lesser criminal was as illogical as it would be to call a little blackness black but a lot white.[2] That this was not just the calm and detached reflection of the philosopher was shown by the life of Mo-tzŭ. Even his critics paid tribute to his passionate and selfless earnestness. To Mencius the teaching of Mo-tzŭ was one of the greatest perils of the time,[3] yet he could say of him 'If by rubbing smooth his whole body from the crown to the heel he could have benefited the kingdom, he would have done it.'[4] A modern Chinese scholar goes even farther and says 'If men had nailed him to a cross, he would certainly not have regretted it, but would have endured it with a smile.'[5] It was not alone in the circle of his disciples that he ventured to teach his principles. When the state of Ch'u was planning an attack on the state of Sung, Mo-tzŭ travelled on foot for ten days and ten nights, tearing his clothes up on the way to bandage his blistered feet, in order to try to

[1] *Mo-tzŭ* xlix (Mei, p. 246; Forke, p. 582; Tomkinson, p. 146).
[2] *Mo-tzŭ* xvii (Mei, pp. 99 f.; Forke, pp. 267 f.; Tomkinson, pp. 60 f.).
[3] *Mencius* III Part 2, ix. 9 f.
[4] *Mencius* VII Part 1, xxvi. 2.
[5] So Liang Ch'i Ch'ao, quoted by S. Holth, *Mencius: a Brief Outline of his Life and Ideas*, 1935, p. 3.

stop the attack.[1] Nor did he trust to pleading alone, but applied his genius to devising defensive plans.

Here he parts company with the Old Testament prophets, who sometimes offered advice and sometimes instigated policies and rebellions by secret action, but who never themselves undertook responsible control of military actions. When the ruler of Sung was indifferent to the moral appeal of Mo-tzŭ, since he believed that a new engine of offence promised him certain victory, Mo-tzŭ demonstrated to the inventor that he could counter it successfully, and when the inventor cherished the ugly thought of eliminating Mo-tzŭ, who lay in his power, the Sage calmly announced that no advantage could be thus gained, since his disciples, primed for their task, were already in the threatened state to aid in its defence.[2] It is impossible to withhold admiration from one who so readily sacrificed and risked his life in the service of others, and whose intrusion into politics was so completely disinterested.[3]

On another occasion, when he sought to dissuade an aggressor from his attack, he found an appeal to moral justification brought against him. The prince observed that in the threatened state the ruler had been assassinated for three generations, and that the disapproval of Heaven had been shown by a three years' famine, so that he was merely acting as the instrument of Heaven in punishing them.[4] Here we are reminded of Isaiah's declaration that the Assyrian was the rod of Yahweh's anger to punish Israel for her defection from Him.[5] Was not the prince of Chêng but making for himself the claim that Isaiah made for the Assyrian? It is improbable that Isaiah would have tolerated such a claim by

---

[1] *Lü Shih Ch'un Ch'iu* XXI, v (cf. R. Wilhelm, *Frühling und Herbst des Lü Bu We*, 1928, pp. 382 f.). For an account of Lü Pu-wei, for whom this work was prepared in the third century B.C., cf. D. Bodde, *Statesman, Patriot and General in Ancient China*, 1940, pp. 1 ff.

[2] *Mo-tzu* l (Mei, pp. 258 f.; Forke, pp. 597 f.; Tomkinson, pp. 154 f.).

[3] Cf. too the tribute to Mo-tzŭ which stands in *Chuang-tzŭ* xxxiii. 2. Here he is described as 'one of the best men in the world, which you may search without finding his equal' (Legge's translation). This is probably one of the spurious chapters of the book (cf. H. A. Giles, *Chuang Tzŭ*, p. 454).

[4] L. Tomkinson, *The Social Teachings of Meh Tse*, p. 145, understands the passage to state that the rulers had been assassinated by their sons.   [5] Isa. x. 5 f.

the king of Assyria, and certainly Mo-tzŭ would not tolerate it from the prince of Chêng. Though to his own people Isaiah could speak of the Assyrian as the rod of Yahweh's anger, he had nothing but condemnation for the Assyrian. He was merely giving vent to the cruel and selfish purpose of his own heart, and was in no sense seeking to serve God, and for his cruel purpose he would be visited with vengeance.[1] So, too, the prince of Chêng was merely giving vent to the aggressive purpose of his own heart, and trying to dress it up in high-sounding terms. 'Suppose', replied Mo-tzŭ, 'there were a man whose son was bad tempered and good for nothing, so that his father thrashed him. If his neighbour's father took up a cudgel and struck him, and said "I am only striking him in accordance with his father's will", would not this be very foolish?'[2] Here, we may note in passing, we have something of the same kind of parabolic appeal to the reason and to conscience which we find, say, in Nathan's parable to David after his adultery with Bathsheba.

Yet again, when Mo-tzŭ sought to dissuade the ruler of the state of Ch'i from attacking the state of Lu, he gave edge to his appeal by observing 'Formerly the king of Wu attacked Yüeh in the east and drove his people to Kuei Chi for refuge. In the west he attacked Ch'u and shut up King Chao in Sui. In the north he attacked Ch'i and took the crown prince[3] prisoner to Wu. Then the nobles exacted vengeance, and his own people were wretched and exhausted and refused to serve him, so that the state came to disaster, and the king himself was executed.'[4] Here, it will be noticed, we have the same implicit recognition of the rightness of revolution and even of regicide that we have found in Confucius and in Mencius, and that was frequently found amongst the prophets of Israel. None of these had any doctrine of the divine right of kings, though all had respect for the office of king. All

[1] Isa. x. 12.

[2] *Mo-tzŭ* xlix (Mei, pp. 245 f.; Forke, pp. 581 f.; Tomkinson, p. 145).

[3] So Forke (*Mê Ti*, p. 579) understands the expression Kuo tzŭ. Mei (*The Works of Motse*, p. 243) understands it to refer to Kuo Shu, a general of the state of Ch'i, while Tomkinson understands the reference to be to one Kuo Tsu Yu.

[4] *Mo-tzŭ* xlix (Mei, pp. 243 f.; Forke, p. 579; Tomkinson, p. 144).

recognized the responsibilities of rulers, as well as the respect that
was due to them, and all were at one in their conviction that the
government existed for the people, and that the well-being of the
people should be its first concern.[1]

Already in the *Shu Ching* we find this principle enunciated.
King Wu is represented as saying that rulers were ordained of God
to help him in His beneficent purposes towards men and to main-
tain the peace of the state, so that when Shou[2] pursued luxury and
extravagance and ruled tyrannically, it became the sacred duty of
Wu to overthrow his dominion.[3] Shou might invoke the principle of the divine right of kings, but Wu could appeal to the
divine right of men to be well governed.

When Confucius was asked about government he replied that
it was essential to put in office men of character and ability,[4] and
in the *Doctrine of the Mean* it is said that the essence of good government was to find the right men.[5] The right man, ordering his own
life aright and developing his own nature as it should be developed,
can help Heaven and Earth by the wise development of the natures
of others. Similarly we find Mo-tzŭ castigating the rulers of his
time because they missed the foundation of true government by
their failure to exalt the virtuous.[6] According to his theory of the
origin of government, it began by the divine selection of the most
virtuous to be emperor, and the emperor's choice of the next in
virtue to be his ministers.[7] As a theory of the origin of government
it has little to commend it; as an ideal of government it has much.

---

[1] Cf. *Mencius* VII Part 2, xiv. 1; 'The people are the most important element in
a nation; the spirits of the land and grain are the next; the sovereign is the lightest.'

[2] Also called Chou.

[3] *Shu Ching* V Book Parts 1-3. The crimes of Shou are expressed in the following words: 'He has been abandoned to drunkenness, and reckless in lust. He has
dared to exercise cruel oppression. Along with criminals he has punished all their
relatives. He has put men into office on the hereditary principle. He has made it
his pursuit to have palaces, towers, pavilions, embankments, ponds, and all other
extravagances, to the most painful injury of you, the myriad people. He has
burned and roasted the loyal and good. He has ripped up pregnant women. Great
Heaven was moved with indignation' (Legge's translation, *The Chinese Classics*,
iii Part 2, 1865, pp. 284 f.).   [4] *Analects* XIII, ii. 1.

[5] *Doctrine of the Mean* xx. 2.   [6] *Mo-tzŭ* viii-x.

[7] *Mo-tzŭ* xiii (Mei, pp. 71 f.; Forke, pp. 231 f.; Tomkinson, pp. 45 f.).

How utterly this contrasts with the indifference of the Taoists! To Chuang-tzŭ it was as foolish to advance the happiness of men as to increase their sorrow, to raise the level of their goodness as to force it down. All government was evil, and the only wisdom lay in letting each live out his own nature.[1] As against this, the prophetic quality of the three Sages at whom we have looked is clear enough. Though there were deep differences between the Confucianists and Mo-tzŭ, and their schools stood in bitter opposition to one another, they were alike in desiring the prevalence of virtue and the well-being of men.

We shall have to consider later the deeper conception of the nature and source of virtue in the thought of the Hebrew prophets. For nothing is farther from my purpose than to equate the Chinese Sages and the Hebrew prophets—unless it is to make the ones the foil for the others. Each group has to be seen in the setting of its own civilization and heritage. In the heritage of Israel there was a more profoundly religious quality, as we shall observe later, but to the Chinese Sages the will of God was the only true basis of human well-being, though they spoke so much less of God than the Hebrews. By their desire for the peace of men, in all the wealth of meaning that the Hebrew word shālôm[2] has, and by their courageous condemnation of the greed and ambition of rulers that impaired that peace, and by their perception that the foundations of that peace were to be found in character, they were men of prophetic spirit and akin to the prophets of Israel, and worthy of our honour.

[1] *Chuang-tzŭ* xi.

[2] On the fullness of meaning of the word *shālôm* cf. J. Pedersen, *Israel I-II*, 1926, pp. 263 ff., 311 ff. On pp. 263 f. Pedersen says: 'This harmony the Israelite calls *shālôm*, the word which is usually rendered by peace. Its fundamental meaning is totality; it means the untrammelled, free growth of the soul. But this, in its turn, means the same as harmonious community; the soul can only expand in conjunction with other souls.' On p. 311 he says: 'In the olden time peace is not in itself the opposite of war. There are friends and there are enemies; peace consists in complete harmony between friends and victory in the war against enemies, for in that consists the full development of the soul. One has "peace" in the fight when one conquers the enemy.'

III

The Prophet as Reformer

IF the Israelite prophets are sometimes referred to as statesmen, they are even more often spoken of as moralists and social reformers. Just as they would have repudiated the description of themselves as statesmen, so they would have repudiated this description, and it is not an adequate one. Nevertheless, there is a measure of truth in it. They were not calm and reflective thinkers, class-room teachers or arm-chair moralists, but men who were alive to the evils of their own day, and who attacked them with passionate vehemence. Their reforming zeal they always attributed to God and not to themselves, but our concern here is not with the source of their zeal, but with its reality and with the forms of its expression.

At the time of the establishment of the monarchy the early prophets, at whom we have more than once looked, were not concerned with social reform. They were concerned for the national survival, and a nation under the heel of another has little opportunity of social reform. Nevertheless, it is quite unjustified to suppose, as is sometimes done, that it was the eighth-century prophets who were first interested in moral and social conditions. When Nathan knew of David's adultery with Bathsheba, he denounced the king's act to his face.[1] This required more courage than Jeremiah's general denunciation of the adulteries that were common in his days,[2] and was evidence of as deep an interest in morals, as well as a championship of the rights of the common

[1] 2 Sam. xii. 7.
[2] Jer. v. 7 f. J. Skinner (*Prophecy and Religion*, 1922, pp. 148 f.) says 'it seems plain that this refers to the morals of the upper class in the capital'. Cf. also Hos. iv. 2.

man against his sovereign. When Ahijah incited Jeroboam to divide the kingdom, both religious and social motives were at work.[1] The prophets saw with concern the steady infiltration of foreign religious and cultural influence owing to Solomon's equal relations with foreign sovereigns, and preferred political insignificance to the submerging of the distinctive religion of Israel beneath the tide of alien influence. But beyond that, they gave expression to the growing discontent of the people as the crown increased its power, and burdens were laid upon them.[2] There might be an advance in civilization, and the court might display a dazzling brilliance and fine buildings go up in Jerusalem; but the price was being paid by the common people. During the reigns of David and Solomon a considerable social revolution had taken place, and it was against this that Ahijah set himself. The once free burghers were reduced to forced labour,[3] and something of the conditions of the Egyptian bondage were being renewed, but with Israelite taskmasters. To the prophets the rights of man were sacred because God willed that they should be his, and any power, whether foreign or Israelite, which infringed those rights must be resisted. Hence Ahijah, supported by other prophets, sought to overthrow the royal power which had encroached so much on the liberties of men, and by political activity succeeded in breaking it.[4] In the northern kingdom, in the time of Ahab, the court was again arrogating to itself powers which aroused the prophets. The methods of Solomon were not

[1] 1 Kings xi. 33. Cf. J. M. P. Smith, *The Prophets and their Times*, 2nd ed., ed. by W. A. Irwin, 1941, pp. 37 f. T. H. Robinson (*A History of Israel*, i, 1932, p. 272) says this narrative may be unhistorical, but is certainly true in other ways. Smith (*loc. cit.*, p. 38), on the other hand, says 'we are fairly safe in accepting this record of Ahijah's participation in the revolt as essentially correct'.

[2] Cf. 1 Kings xii. 4.   [3] 1 Kings v. 13 ff. (Heb. 27 ff.).

[4] T. H. Robinson (*op. cit.*, i, pp. 272 f.) says: 'The prophets . . . stood for a pure Yahwism, and, drawn as they normally were from the proletariat and the unofficial classes, they strongly maintained the popular view of society, law and politics. We have no other instance of a class of men in any state in the ancient east who thus represented the common people and were at the same time immune from royal punishment owing to their sanctity. We cannot doubt that . . . they maintained the strongly democratic spirit which the Aramaean invaders had brought into the land.'

being renewed, but by subtler means the alien queen Jezebel exerted her influence to sweep Naboth,[1] with his insistence on his rights, out of Ahab's way, and to silence the prophets whom she feared.[2] But one rugged figure she could not sweep from her path. This was the prophet Elijah, who was concerned for Naboth, and for much more than Naboth. He was concerned for the rights of the common man, and for the social health of the nation.

It was no new thing, therefore, when the eighth-century prophets showed a profound interest in moral and social conditions. Again a social revolution had taken place or was in process of taking place, and they were actively interested. The aggressive influences now were not merely the court, but various classes of the people who were exploiting their power over others, and creating deeper cleavages and profound dissatisfaction. It is true that the eighth-century prophets did not resort to political intrigue, as Ahijah and Elisha did, but confined themselves to public protest in the name of God. But their concern to fight against all infringement of the rights of men, and their interest in the social and moral conditions of their day were not fundamentally different from the concern and interest of their predecessors.

In the first half of the eighth century there was an expansion of wealth in both of the Israelite states. The power of Damascus had been broken and a period of little Assyrian activity in the west down to the middle of the century followed. This situation presented an opportunity of peaceful development which brought to both kingdoms the growth of material resources.[3] In the time of Solomon such growth had been concentrated largely in the hands of the king; now it was concentrated in the hands of a section of society. Many of the peasants became poorer, and the rich became richer, so that an ever-widening gap separated the rich from the poor. Amos gives us some insight into the situation in the northern kingdom in the time of Jeroboam II, and from

---

[1] 1 Kings xxi. 8 ff.
[2] 1 Kings xviii. 4, 13; xix. 10, 14.
[3] Cf. E. G. H. Kraeling, *Aram and Israel*, 1918, pp. 83 f.; Robinson, *A History of Israel*, i, p. 358.

Isaiah and Micah we find that similar conditions were still found in the southern kingdom towards the end of the century.

Instead of the peasant landholders of former times a class of large estate holders was coming into being. Isaiah denounces those who join lands to lands,[1] and already in Amos we see evidences of the same situation. A poor year might drive the peasants to borrow money to tide them over until the harvest, and the creditors ruthlessly exploited their power. Presumably the security offered would be the growing crops, but it was customary for the borrower's cloak to be deposited with the lender as a pledge. Since he would possess but one cloak, this would prevent him from getting loans on the same security from more than one creditor. The lack of the cloak would be no hardship to him in the daytime, when he was working, but at night he would need it for a covering, and it was the custom for it to be returned to him nightly for this purpose.[2] The creditors were so lacking in humanity, however, that they often withheld the pledge,[3] and this inflicted on the borrower a real hardship which Amos denounced. We are not told the rates of interest that prevailed, but they were doubtless high. During the years that I lived in China reputable Chinese banks paid as much as 10 per cent interest on fixed deposits, and the sort of rates of interest which they charged may be surmised. I knew a Chinese who put aside more than $100 a month from his salary and lent it out on interest, and another Chinese who knew him well assured me that he charged 3 per cent per month by way of interest. What the rates in eighth-century Israel were we have no means of knowing, but if they were of anything like this order, it would be difficult for a peasant who had once got involved in debt to extricate himself. Some mishap to the growing crops—such as the locust plague which Joel in a much later age describes[4] —would put him wholly at the mercy of the creditor, while a much less misfortune would tighten the grip upon him, until he was reduced to the position of a serf on the land he once

---

[1] Isa. v. 8; cf. Mic. ii. 2.
[3] Amos ii. 8.
[2] Exod. xxii. 26 f.
[4] Joel i. 4 ff.

possessed,[1] cultivating for the man from whom he had borrowed money, and paying into his pocket the lion's share of all he should henceforth earn. The Israelites were no longer a brotherhood, members of a common covenant, but voracious landlords and their impoverished victims. Greed had extinguished humanity, and every misfortune was exploited to the utmost. The widow and the fatherless stirred no pity,[2] and their helpless state was quickly turned to the enrichment of others.

Nor was this all. For most of this it might be pleaded that though it was hard, it was legitimate. The creditor was not responsible for the misfortunes. But greed did not stop there. The processes of justice were also exploited and the courts were turned into the instruments of gross injustice. By the offering of bribes to the judges verdicts were obtained against those who were in no position to offer bribes, and injustice was added to misfortune to make the lot of the poor more miserable.[3]

Meanwhile the rich flaunted their wealth. They lived in splendid and richly adorned houses, feasting and drinking,[4] and resorting to the shrines there to display their religiosity in splendid sacrifices.[5] Yet even their worship was tainted with their immoralities. For the practices of the Canaanite fertility cult still survived and ritual prostitution went on in the shrines.[6] To the prophets this was nothing but fornication, and it provided Hòsea with a metaphor to describe Israel's disloyalty to God.[7]

In varying ways and in varying terms all the eighth-century prophets whose oracles have come down to us denounced these things, and pronounced woes on those who were responsible for

[1] Amos viii. 4 ff., Mic. ii. 2. The passage in Amos indicates that commercial dishonesty was added to the other forms of exploitation.

[2] Isa. i. 17, 23, x. 2.   [3] Amos ii. 6, viii. 6, Isa. i. 23, v. 23, Mic. ii. 11.

[4] Amos iii. 15, vi. 4 ff.; cf. Hos. iv. 11. For the condemnation of drunkenness cf. *Shu Ching* V Book 10.

[5] Amos v. 21 ff., Isa. i. 11.

[6] Amos ii. 7 probably refers to this. Cf. S. R. Driver, *The Books of Joel and Amos*, 2nd ed., edited by H. C. O. Lanchester, 1915, p. 153: 'The allusion is in all probability not to common immorality, but to immorality practised in the precincts of a temple.'

[7] Hos. iv. 15, v. 3 f., vi. 10.

them.[1] The rottenness of society was bound to lead to disaster. For these things were an offence against God, as well as against man. The very worship offered to Him was an offence to Him, since it was offered by men who in their lives proclaimed their scorn for the character of God. Isaiah declared that the hands which they lifted in prayer to Him were stained with the blood of their victims.[2] The blood of Abel had cried to God from the ground;[3] but they flaunted in His face the blood of men and came to Him fresh from their iniquities.[4] Yet to Isaiah the Temple in Jerusalem was always the House of God, sacred and inviolable, and though men defiled it He would yet preserve it, and Jerusalem for its sake.[5] In the days of Isaiah so it was. But his contemporary Micah yet more sharply denounced the evils of his day, and declared that the very Temple would be destroyed because of those evils.[6]

A century later Jeremiah found conditions in Jerusalem no better. The wicked lurked like fowlers for their fellow men, and grew sleek through their iniquities.[7] He declared that in the whole city of Jerusalem it was impossible to find one who loved justice and truth.[8] Corruption had invaded the lives of men to such a pitch that adultery was common,[9] and oppression rampant.[10]

---

[1] Micah declares that the cruel oppression of man by man was equivalent to cannibalism. He declaims against those 'who hate the good, and love the evil; who pluck off their skin from off them, and their flesh from off their bones; who also eat the flesh of my people; and they flay their skin from off them, and break their bones: yea, they chop them in pieces, as for the pot, and as flesh within the cauldron' (Mic. iii. 2 f.).

[2] Isa. i. 15.   [3] Gen. iv. 10.

[4] Cf. also Isa. v. 7: 'he looked for judgement, but behold oppression (R.V. marg. shedding of blood); for righteousness, but behold a cry'. Here there is a play on words in the Hebrew between mishpāṭ=judgement, and mispāḥ=bloodshed, and between ṣedhāḳāh=righteousness, and ṣeʿāḳāh=cry.

[5] Cf. Isa. iv. 5 f., xxxi. 5, xxxiii. 20 ff.

[6] Mic. iii. 12.   ·   [7] Jer. v. 26 ff.

[8] Jer. v. 1. Truth is here something more than accuracy of statement. L. E. Binns, The Book of the Prophet Jeremiah, 1919, p. 49, observes that it 'includes faithfulness towards God and justice towards men'. Cf. F. Asensio, Misericordia et Veritas, 1949, pp. 275 f.

[9] Jer. v. 8: cf. Hos. iv. 4.   [10] Jer. vii. 6 ff.

Justice was still a stranger to the courts and the fatherless aroused no pity.[1]

It would be easy to multiply references to the prophets to show their indignation at the conditions of their day. They did not deal in moral maxims, but in hot anger at the concrete evils of their times. What they demanded of men was summed up in familiar words as to do justly, to love mercy, and to walk humbly with God.[2] By mercy something more than compassion is meant. It was the quality which God had shown towards Israel, a quality in which grace, generosity and unwavering loyalty were united. It involved a profound devotion that counted no service too great, and that demanded only by what it gave. It was not to the flinty justice of Shylock they summoned men, but to a justice tempered by this quality of *hesedh*—never demanding more than its right, and tempering its demand by a warm and gracious spirit that reflected the spirit of God. It was to a genuine spirit of brotherhood that should pervade the whole of society.[3]

When now we pass to the Chinese sages we find many differences, but many similarities. T. H. Robinson says 'There is a certain sense in which every reformer is the product and representative of his age.'[4] The Chinese sages lived in a very different age from the Hebrews and are necessarily very different persons. Yet they too were deeply interested in the social conditions of their time and sought to effect changes. Their ideals for society differed notably from those of the Old Testament prophets; but they were nevertheless prophets, who proclaimed what they believed to be the will of God for society, and who attacked the evils of their day in their own way. They enunciated their principles to kings and princes, or to their own disciples, and sought to change society from the top. But they were deeply concerned for the well-being of the common man.

---

[1] Jer. v. 28.   [2] Mic. vi. 8.

[3] A. Lods, *The Prophets and the Rise of Judaism*, E.Tr. by S. H. Hooke, 1937, p. 89, defines *hesedh* as 'a very comprehensive word, which, for want of an adequate equivalent, we are obliged to translate, now by piety, now by mercy, love, or grace: it corresponded fairly closely to the Latin *pietas*'. He adds 'Cf. *hsiao* in the doctrine of Confucius.'   [4] *Prophecy and the Prophets*, p. 60.

Mencius describes the times of Confucius by saying that the world had fallen into decay, and perverse doctrines and violent deeds were rife. Ministers murdered their sovereigns and sons their fathers. Confucius was afraid, and wrote the *Ch'un Ch'iu*.[1] The effect of this work, Mencius goes on to add, was that rebellious ministers and villainous sons were terror-stricken.[2] In its record of the 234 years before the birth of Confucius the *Ch'un Ch'iu* records thirty-six cases of regicide.[3] In the appendix to the *Book of Changes*, or *I Ching*, we read 'The murder of a ruler by his minister, or of a father by his son, is not the result of the events of one morning or one evening. The causes of it have gradually accumulated.'[4] On this Hu Shih comments 'The cause of the moral and political disorder lies deeper than such unnatural acts as regicide and parricide themselves. There has been a long and gradual process of intellectual disorganization, decadence of beliefs and convictions, and relaxation of duties and relations.'[5] It was to this situation that Confucius addressed himself, not alone by the writing of the *Ch'un Ch'iu*, but by much of his teaching.

The dry annals of the *Ch'un Ch'iu* have nothing of the character of the prophetic utterances of the prophets of Israel, and to the simple reader they contain little to strike terror into any reader. Their edge lay in the precision of the terms used. Hu Shih cites a number of examples of the annals relating to regicide.[6] In some the name of the regicide is given and the term used is *shih*, *assassinated*. In one of the cases cited we find the term *sha*, *killed*, to indicate the judgement of Confucius that this was a legitimate act,

---

[1] *Mencius* III Part 2, ix. 7 f. According to tradition it was near the end of his life that Confucius wrote the *Ch'un Ch'iu*. Cf. R. Wilhelm, *Confucius and Confucianism*, E.Tr., p. 128.

[2] *Mencius* III Part 2, ix. 11.

[3] Cf. Hu Shih, *The Development of the Logical Method in Ancient China*, p. 22.

[4] Appendix IV, ii. 5 (translation of Legge in *The Sacred Books of the East*, xvi, 2nd ed., 1899, pp. 419 f.). The *I Ching* has also been translated in rearranged form in R. Wilhelm, *The I Ching, or Book of Changes*, E.Tr. by C. F. Baynes, 2 vols., 1951.

[5] *Op. cit.*, p. 23.

[6] *Op. cit.*, pp. 50 f. Cf. also R. Wilhelm, *Confucius and Confucianism*, E.Tr., pp. 130 f.

since the victim deserved his fate.[1] In one case the murderer is stigmatized as the heir apparent, to mark his crime as the more
heinous. In one case the murder is attributed to the uncle of the
actual murderer, because he failed as prime minister to bring his
nephew to justice. All this is in accordance with Confucius's
teaching that the first thing to do in reforming the administration
of the government was to rectify names.[2] When names and realities
corresponded, and the ugly deed was called by the ugly name,
Confucius believed that men would amend their ways. When
moral distinctions are confused by an abuse of language, men are
misled. This was perceived by Isaiah, who cried 'Woe to those
who call good evil and evil good.'[3] Different as the method of
Confucius was, therefore, a prophetic purpose inspired his work.

As has been said, Confucius sought to reform society from the
top. He had an excessive faith in the power of example,[4] and
believed that if rulers were themselves of exemplary virtue and
conducted the government on correct principles all else could take
care of itself. 'He who exercises government by means of his
virtue may be compared to the north polar star, which keeps its
place and all the stars turn towards it,' he said.[5] Or again, 'To
govern means to rectify.[6] If you lead on the people with correct-
ness, who will dare not to be correct?'[7] On another occasion he
observed 'If the people be led by laws, and uniformity sought to
be given them by punishments, they will try to avoid the punishment, but have no sense of shame. If they be led by virtue, and

---

[1] Cf. *Mencius* I Part 2, viii. 3, where the king of Ch'i uses the word *shih* of King
Wu's removal of Chou and Mencius substitutes the word *chu*—a synonym of
sha—to indicate that in his view this was not regicide but legitimate punishment
of one who had forfeited his right to be king. Legge renders: 'I have heard of the
cutting off (*chu*) of the fellow Châu, but I have not heard of the putting a sovereign
to death.'

[2] *Analects* XIII, iii. On this passage see above, p. 18 n.   [3] Isa. v. 20.

[4] Cf. *Analects* IV, xxv, XII, xviii; cf. also *Great Learning*, Commentary x. 21.
It is, of course, undoubted that there is power in example, though it is not so
invincible as Confucius supposed. Shang Yang says: 'The benevolent may be
benevolent towards others, but cannot cause others to be benevolent; the righteous
may love others, but cannot cause others to love' (iv. 18, translation of Duyvendak, *The Book of Lord Shang*, 1928, p. 293).   [5] *Analects* II, i.

[6] Here there is a play on words: *Chêng chê chêng yeh.*   [7] *Analects* XII, xvii.

uniformity be given them by the rules of propriety, they will have the sense of shame, and moreover will become good.'[1]

It is fair to remember that the evils of society in his day had their source in the ambitions of princes, and that he, like the prophets of Israel, was addressing himself to the evils of his time and not composing a text-book on the art of government. Judge him in relation to the world in which he lived, and it will appear that the ideals which he set before the rulers offered some real way of mitigating the evils. 'To rule a country of a thousand chariots,' he said, 'there must be reverent attention to business, and sincerity; economy in expenditure, and love for men; and the employment of the people at the proper seasons.'[2] Some of this would be highly commended if we read it in the Old Testament as uttered to Solomon; it was no less worthy when it was uttered to reach the ears of rulers whose administration was a flagrant repudiation of these principles.

On another occasion Confucius is said to have commended as the principles of wise government beneficence with economy, the imposing on the people only of burdens which they did not resent, the avoidance of covetousness, dignity without pride, and majesty without harshness.[3] On the other hand the evils to be avoided were said to be the putting of people to death without first instructing them, the imposing of oppressive burdens without warning, arbitrary pressure upon subjects, and meanness in rewarding service.[4] Isaiah might have expressed this in a series of vigorous woes; but it should be clear that Confucius was addressing himself to the social evils of his age in his own way.

When asked how to secure the willing obedience of the people, he replied 'Advance the upright and set aside the crooked.'[5] Character was the first essential for public service in the eyes of

---

[1] *Analects* II, iii.   [2] *Analects* I, v.

[3] *Analects* XX, ii. 1. Book XX of the *Analects* is of doubtful authenticity (cf. A. Waley, *The Analects of Confucius*, p. 25), and can only be used with caution. The substance here is in close accord with that of the passage referred to in the preceding note and with that of some other passages, so that it may legitimately be used for corroboration here.

[4] *Analects* XX, ii. 3.   [5] *Analects* II, xix. Cf. also XII, xxii. 3.

Confucius, and it is when we look at his teaching in contrast to that of the Taoist teachers that we can appreciate its worth. Lieh-tzŭ[1] records with apparent approval the commendation by Têng Hsi of the sentiments of one who said: 'He who is bent on putting the world around him in order cannot be certain that the world will accept his rule, but may be sure that his own life will be disagreeable. He who is bent only upon enjoying life cannot be certain that the world will therefore be disordered, but he may be sure that he himself will be a great deal more comfortable.'[2] Têng Hsi was not himself a Taoist, but the father of the Legalists,[3] and how far he was from the spirit of Confucius, with his demand for benevolence and consideration for the subjects, may be seen from his teaching that the prince ought to treat his people without shadow of kindness or pity, but with the utmost rigour.[4]

It would be very unfair to Confucius, however, to give the impression that he was concerned only with the ruler. He believed that if the ruler set a right example it would be followed down through society, but he was careful also to set his ideals for all classes forth in his teaching. When he said 'Riches and honour acquired by unrighteousness are to me as a floating cloud',[5] he was condemning grasping avarice in subjects no less than in princes. Righteousness was more than wealth to Confucius, as it was to the prophets of Israel. When Amos condemned the splendid sacrifices offered by the oppressive rich of his day he demanded that righteousness should flow like a never-failing

[1] On Lieh-tzŭ cf. Forke, *Geschichte der alten chinesischen Philosophie*, pp. 284 ff.; Wieger, *Histoire des Croyances religieuses*, pp. 157 ff.; L. Giles, *Taoist Teachings*, 1912, pp. 13 ff.

[2] *Lieh-tzŭ* vii (translation of A. Waley, *Three Ways of Thought in Ancient China*, 1939, p. 50). A translation of *Lieh-tzŭ* may also be found in L. Wieger, *Taoïsme*, ii, 1913, pp. 69 ff. (accompanied by Chinese text), and of chapter vii (with Chinese text) in Legge, *The Chinese Classics*, ii, 2nd ed., pp. 93 ff. A German translation may be found in R. Wilhelm, *Liä Dsi*, 1921. Cf. also A. Forke, *Yang Chu's Garden of Pleasure*, 1912.

[3] On Têng Hsi cf. Forke, *op. cit.*, pp. 418 ff.; Wieger, *Histoire des Croyances religieuses*, pp. 231 ff.

[4] Cf. Wieger, *op. cit.*, p. 234.

[5] *Analects* VII, xv. Waley renders: 'Any thought of accepting wealth and rank by means that I know to be wrong is as remote from me as clouds that float above.'

river through the life of the nation,[1] and Confucius could well have echoed this demand. 'When a country is ill governed,' he said, 'riches and honour are things to be ashamed of.'[2]

While the Commentary on the *Great Learning* cannot be ascribed to Confucius, it reflects his ideas and teaching when it declares 'Never has there been a case of the sovereign loving benevolence, and the people not loving righteousness. Never has there been a case where the people had loved righteousness, and the affairs of the sovereign have not been carried to completion.'[3] Nor was the virtue of the sovereign to be expressed only in the affairs of the state, but also in his private relations. In the same Commentary on the *Great Learning* propriety in their relations with the aged and with the young is demanded of sovereigns, and the consequence is promised in propriety of behaviour throughout all classes of society. This propriety of conduct is presented as a measuring square for all classes.[4]

Propriety alone is a very inadequate definition of the demand of Confucius on men,[5] and though it played an important part in his conception of the duty of man, it was by no means his complete panacea for the ills of society. 'Hold faithfulness and sincerity as first principles' was one of his fundamental demands of men.[6] These were qualities of universal application, and they are comparable with the demands of the Old Testament prophets for qualities of character as the only satisfying solution to the social problems of their day. 'The man who in view of gain thinks of righteousness; who in view of danger is prepared to give up his life; and who does not forget an old agreement however far back it extends—such a man may be reckoned a complete man,' said Confucius.[7] Yet in this definition of the 'complete man' there is wanting an element which is characteristic of the teaching of the

---

[1] Amos v. 24. [2] *Analects* VIII, xiii. 3.

[3] *The Great Learning*, Commentary x. 21.

[4] *The Great Learning*, Commentary x. 1.

[5] L. Giles (*The Sayings of Confucius*, 1949 ed., p. 60 n.) writes scornfully of those who make the sayings of Confucius 'to suggest nothing so much as the headmistress of a young ladies' seminary'.

[6] *Analects* I, viii. 2, IX, xxiv, XII, x. 1. [7] *Analects* XIV, xiii. 2.

Sage. This is the element of reciprocity. When asked whether there was one word which could serve as a rule of practice for all life, he replied 'Is not reciprocity such a word? What you do not want done to yourself, do not do to others.'[1] Or again, when asked about perfect virtue,[2] part of his definition was expressed in the words 'not to do to others as you would not wish done to yourself'.[3] One of his disciples declared that his teaching could be wholly summed up in the words faithfulness and reciprocity,[4] and the Commentary on the *Great Learning* says that no man can instruct others who has not learned to apply the principle of reciprocity and to measure men by the same standard which he applies to himself.[5] In an age of selfishness and decay such as that of

[1] *Analects* XV, xxiii. Cf. also *Chia Yü* II, 11 b, 12 a, Section ix, §1 (Kramers, *K'ung Tzŭ Chia Yü*, pp. 239 f.).

[2] *Jên*, which Legge renders elsewhere by *benevolence*, or *humanity*. Z. K. Zia (*The Confucian Civilization*, 1925, pp. 30 ff.) complains that Legge renders this word in a variety of ways. Like the Hebrew word *ḥesedh*, it has no single equivalent in English, and Zia admits this (p. 34). Cf. A. Waley, *The Analects of Confucius*, pp. 27 ff., where it is held that in the *Analects* it should be rendered by *Good* or *Goodness* (the capital letter distinguishing it from *shan*, which is rendered by *good*). Kramers (*K'ung Tzŭ Chia Yü*, p. 211) uses a small g for *jên* when he renders: 'In goodness nothing is greater than to love others.' Cf. also Granet (*La pensée chinoise*, 1934, p. 486) on the meaning of this word.   [3] *Analects* XII, ii.

[4] *Analects* IV, xv. 2. The translation of Legge here conceals the use of the word *shu*, which is elsewhere rendered by *reciprocity*. Legge has 'The doctrine of our Master is to be true to the principles of our nature and the benevolent exercise of them to others—this and nothing more.' In the Chinese text there are eight words which may be more simply rendered, in accordance with Legge's usage elsewhere, 'The Master's teaching is wholly summed up in faithfulness (*chung*) and reciprocity (*shu*).' Waley has 'Our Master's Way is simply this: Loyalty, consideration,' while Lyall has: 'The Master's Way is no more than faithfulness and fellow-feeling.' L. Giles (*The Saying of Confucius*, p. 69 n.) says the word *shu* 'is almost equivalent to *jên*, goodness of heart, only with the idea of *altruism* more explicitly brought out. It connotes sympathetic consideration for others, and hence the best rendering would seem to be "loving-kindness" or "charity" .' In the above cited *Analects* XV, xxiii, Soothill uses *sympathy*.

[5] *The Great Learning*, Commentary ix. 4. Here, once more, Legge's translation conceals the use of the word *shu = reciprocity*. Legge renders 'Never has there been a man, who, not having reference to his own character and wishes in dealing with others, was able effectually to instruct them,' where Couvreur has 'Un homme qui ne sait pas mesurer et traiter les autres avec la même mesure que lui-même, ne peut pas les instruire.' It will be seen that Couvreur brings out the element of reciprocity which is indicated in the Chinese by the use of the word *shu*.

Confucius, high honour belonged to the teacher who could issue such a call to men.

I have elsewhere argued[1] that the teaching of Confucius was far superior to the oft-quoted saying of the *Tao Tê Ching* 'Recompense injury with kindness.'[2] Taken out of its context this may seem a noble maxim, and the specific repudiation of it by Confucius is often held to put Confucius on a lower plane. But in the light of its context and of the whole teaching of the *Tao Tê Ching* it is clear that it really expressed a supreme indifference to others, and was vastly inferior to Confucius's profound interest in men. Confucius said 'They who return kindness for injury are such as have a regard for their own persons',[3] and a modern scholar has observed that the maxim in the *Tao Tê Ching* 'is no more than a precept of indifferent self-possession' and that its meaning is no more than 'Be a Taoist, even though provoked.'[4]

How inferior to the teaching of Confucius is that of the *Tao Tê Ching* is very clear from another passage, where we read: 'Heaven and earth do not act from any wish to be benevolent; they deal with all things as the dogs of grass[5] are dealt with. The sages do not act from any wish to be benevolent; they deal with the people

---

[1] Cf. *Submission in Suffering*, pp. 77 ff., 82 ff.

[2] *Tao Tê Ching* lxiii. The word here rendered by *kindness* is normally rendered by *virtue*, and Duyvendak here renders: 'By requiting grievances with virtue.' In closer accord with Legge's rendering Waley gives: 'Requite injuries with good deeds,' while L. Giles (*The Sayings of Lao Tzŭ*, 1917 ed., p. 51) agrees with Legge. Duyvendak transfers this saying from chapter lxiii to chapter lxxix, where it then provides the answer to the question 'How can one stand well with others?'

[3] Cf. *Li Chi* xxix. 12. Cheng T'ien-hsi (*China Moulded by Confucius*, 1946, pp. 80 f.) objects to Legge's rendering here, and renders 'To recompense injury with kindness is a virtue of magnanimity.' This does not appear to suit the context, though it is to be noted that the Chinese text has *jên=benevolence*, where Legge, following the Chinese commentators, reads *jên=man*. S. Couvreur (*Li Ki*, ii, 1899, p. 484) renders: 'Celui qui rend le bien pour le mal se fait du bien à lui-même par sa bonté (parce qu'on aime à lui rendre service),' while R. Wilhelm, *Li Gi*, 1930, p. 152) renders: 'Wer Hass mit Liebe vergilt, der schafft seiner eigenen Güte einen breiten Wirkungskreis.'

[4] P. J. Maclagan, in Hastings's *E.R.E.*, xii, 1921, p. 199 a.

[5] I.e. straw dogs used in ritual acts and then cast aside and burned.

as the dogs of grass are dealt with.'[1] Duyvendak thinks this passage was a polemic against the Confucian inculcation of humanity or benevolence.[2] The judgement of Wieger would seem to be fully justified: 'Nothing of morality enters into this brutal system. . . . It is physical, blind, immutable, eternal law.'[3] Moreover, Duyvendak underlines the close connection between the teaching of the *Tao Tê Ching* and that of the school of Legalists.[4] Both urged that the people should be kept in ignorance and should be set to constant hard work. I am not disposed to share the frequently expressed view that the author of the *Tao Tê Ching* was superior to Confucius.

Nor is it fair to lay emphasis on the negative character of Confucius's definition of reciprocity 'What you do not want done to yourself, do not do to others.' In the *Doctrine of the Mean* the maxim is quoted in this negative form, and then the author continues 'In the way of the superior man there are four things, to not one of which have I as yet attained. To serve my father, as I would require my son to serve me . . .; to serve my prince, as I would require my minister to serve me . . .; to serve my elder brother, as I would require my younger brother to serve me . . .; to set the example in behaving to a friend, as I would require him to behave to me.'[5] Here we find a positive enunciation of the principle, which is not unfaithful to the spirit of Confucius.

In Confucius we do not find the passionate championing of the poor and helpless that we find in the prophets of Israel, but we must acknowledge a genuinely prophetic message and a profound desire to eradicate some of the crying evils of the society of his day. There were differences of emphasis between the Hebrew prophets, and no one of them gave utterance to the full demand which is found in the total teaching of them all, and I am not disposed to depreciate Confucius for the lack of this or that element, but to recognize the greatness of the man who addressed himself

---

[1] *Tao Tê Ching* v. This passage is included by L. Giles in *The Sayings of Lao Tzŭ*, p. 43.

[2] Cf. *Tao Te Ching*, 1954, p. 28.   [3] *Histoire des Croyances religieuses*, p. 150.

[4] *Op. cit.*, pp. 12 f.   [5] *The Doctrine of the Mean* xiii. 3 f.

to the colossal task of reforming by moral suasion such a society as that into which he was born.

In the teaching of Mencius there is nothing that goes beyond the thought of Confucius on the subjects now before us. He rarely uses the word *shu*, or *reciprocity*, which was one of the key words of Confucius. In one passage, which Legge describes as mystical, we find the word, where Legge translates: 'If one acts with a vigorous effort at the law of reciprocity, when he seeks for the realization of perfect virtue (*jên*), nothing can be closer than his approximation to it.'[1] He, too, sought to reform society from the top, and insisted with greater emphasis on the duty of the ruler to infuse his government with humanity and to treat his subjects with consideration.[2] When one of the princes asked him to advise how the state might be profited, Mencius at once dismissed the word 'profit', and declared that what mattered was that the government should be inspired by benevolence and righteousness. If the king was concerned for his own profit, then the same desire for profit would run through all society, and naked selfishness would reign. 'Let your Majesty say "Benevolence and righteousness shall be the only themes." Why must you speak of profit?' said Mencius.[3] In similar terms Mencius rebuked one who proposed to dissuade two princes from going to war by appealing to the motive of profit. 'If you, starting from the point of profit,' said Mencius, 'offer your persuasive counsels to the kings of Ts'in and Ts'oo, and if those kings are pleased with the consideration of profit so as to stop the movements of their armies, then all belonging to those armies will rejoice in the cessation of war, and find their pleasure in the pursuit of profit. Ministers will serve their sovereign for the profit of which they cherish the thought; sons will serve their fathers, and younger brothers will serve their elder brothers, from the same consideration; and the issue will be that, abandoning benevolence and righteousness, sovereign and ministers, father and son, brother and elder, will carry on all their intercourse with this thought of profit cherished in their breasts.

[1] *Mencius* VII Part I, iv. 3.   [2] *Mencius* I Part I, iii. 4.
[3] *Mencius* I Part I, i. 6.

But never has there been such a state of society without ruin being the result of it.'[1]

Nor was Mencius content to speak of benevolence as an abstract term. He gave it concrete content in terms which made clear his interest in the common man. In this he was nearer to the Israelite prophets than Confucius, and it is clear that the sufferings of ordinary men and women in the incessant wars of the time aroused his profound sympathy. To another prince the Sage said 'Now the livelihood of the people is so regulated that above they have not sufficient wherewith to serve their parents, and below they have not sufficient to support their wives and children. Notwithstanding good years their lives are continually embittered, and in bad years they do not escape perishing. In such circumstances they only try to save themselves from death, and are afraid they will not succeed. What leisure have they to cultivate propriety and righteousness?'[2] On another occasion he said to the first of the princes mentioned above 'Your dogs and swine eat the food of men, and you do not know to make any restrictive arrangements. There are people dying from famine on the roads, and you do not know to issue the stores of your granaries for them. When people die, you say, "It is not owing to me; it is owing to the year." In what does this differ from stabbing a man and killing him, and then saying, "It was not I; it was the weapon"?'[3] He continued 'In your kitchen there is fat meat; in your stables there are fat horses. But your people have the look of hunger, and on the wilds there are those who have died of famine. This is leading on beasts to devour men. Beasts devour one another, and men hate them for doing so. When a prince, being the parent of his people, administers his government so as to be chargeable with leading on beasts to devour men, where is the parental relation to the people?'[4]

On yet another occasion Mencius observed that when the people heard the royal music and hunting parties they were so immersed in their own miseries that they merely observed 'That's how our king likes to enjoy himself', whereas if he were concerned

[1] *Mencius* VI Part 2, iv. 5.   [2] *Mencius* I Part I, vii. 22.
[3] *Mencius* I Part I, iii. 5.   [4] *Mencius* I Part I, iv. 4 f.

for their well-being they would rejoice in his pleasures and would say 'That sounds as if the king is in good health.'[1]

Like Confucius Mencius believed that if only things were right at the top everything would be well. 'Let the prince be correct', he said, 'and everything will be correct. Once rectify the prince, and the kingdom will be firmly settled.'[2] Or again 'If the sovereign be benevolent, all will be benevolent. If the sovereign be righteous, all will be righteous.'[3] At the same time he insisted that benevolence must be not alone felt but put into practice. 'Virtue alone is not sufficient for the government,' he quoted with approval; 'Laws alone cannot carry themselves into practice.'[4] Like Confucius again Mencius valued righteousness and propriety. 'I like life and I also like righteousness', he said. 'If I cannot keep the two together, I will let life go, and choose righteousness. I like life indeed, but there is that which I like more than life, and therefore I will not seek to possess it by improper ways. I dislike death indeed, but there is that which I dislike more than death, and therefore there are occasions when I will not avoid danger.'[5] As to propriety, Mencius commended a forester who failed to answer the summons of his ducal master in the hunt, because he was summoned by a flag and not by the correct fur cap.[6] Arising from this Mencius enunciated the principle, which might have found better illustration, 'Never has a man who has bent himself been able to make others straight.'[7]

He shared Confucius's faith in the unlimited power of virtue. 'Among the shepherds of men throughout the empire', he said, 'there is not one who does not find pleasure in killing men. If there were one who did not find pleasure in killing men, all the people in the empire would look towards him with out-stretched necks. Such being indeed the case, the people would flock to him, as water flows downwards with a rush, which no one can repress.'[8]

[1] *Mencius* I Part 2, i. 6 f.　　　　[2] *Mencius* IV Part 1, xx.
[3] *Mencius* IV Part 2, v.　　　　[4] *Mencius* IV Part 1, i. 3.
[5] *Mencius* VI Part 1, x. 1 f.　　　　[6] *Mencius* III Part 2, i. 2.
[7] *Mencius* III Part 2, i. 5. With this we may compare the saying of Confucius: 'If a minister cannot rectify himself, what has he to do with rectifying others?' (*Analects* XIII, xiii).　　　　[8] *Mencius* I Part 1, vi. 6.

In reply to the question 'What virtue must there be in order to the attainment of imperial sway?' he answered 'The love and protection of the people; with this there is no power which can prevent a ruler from attaining it.'[1] Or again, shortly after, 'If your Majesty will institute a government whose action shall all be benevolent, this will cause all the officers in the empire to wish to stand in your Majesty's court, and the farmers all to wish to plough in your Majesty's fields, and the merchants, both travelling and stationary, all wish to store their goods in your Majesty's market places, and travelling strangers all wish to make their tours on your Majesty's roads, and all throughout the empire who feel aggrieved by their rulers to wish to come and complain to your Majesty. And when they are so bent, who will be able to keep them back?'[2]

A bolder and blunter note is thus struck by Mencius, and his compassion for the common people appears to have been stronger than Confucius's, and to this extent he stands a little nearer to the Israelite prophets. But his prophetic message was not essentially different from that of Confucius, in whom he found his inspiration.

In Mo-tzŭ the spirit of compassion for the common people in their sufferings and the sense of urgent need for radical reforms was even stronger. The luxury and extravagance of his day moved him as a comparable situation moved the eighth-century prophets, and he demanded a puritanic austerity of life that has brought on him much condemnation from those who forget the times in which he lived. In public affairs he advocated a rigid economy of expenditure. 'To cut out useless expenditure', he declared, 'was the way of the Sage-Kings,'[3] and elsewhere he says 'Whatever adds to expense but adds nothing to the profit of the people, the Sage-Kings did not countenance.'[4] He similarly declaims against the contemporary waste in private expenditure. The tyranny of custom which demanded heavy expense on funerals

---

[1] *Mencius* I Part I, vii. 3.   [2] *Mencius* I Part I, vii. 18.
[3] *Mo-tzŭ* xx (Mei, p. 119; Forke, p. 292; Tomkinson, p. 73).
[4] *Mo-tzŭ* xxi (Mei, p. 122; Forke, p. 296; Tomkinson, p. 75).

came under his attack. Peasants were reduced to poverty and the funeral of a nobleman, he declared, was costly enough to empty the treasury of the state.[1] A coffin three inches thick should suffice, said Mo-tzŭ, the shroud should be simple, the grave not unduly deep, the period of mourning should end with the interment, and work should be resumed.[2]

He was resolutely opposed to music,[3] which Confucius had exalted as essential to the life of the princely man.[4] But it is fair that we should remember that by music Mo-tzŭ meant more than we mean by the term. 'The term is applied', says Z. L. Yih, 'to engravings, delicious food and beautiful houses. In fact it means all sorts of luxuries, arts and pleasure-seeking,'[5] while Arthur Waley observes 'What Mo-tzŭ had in mind were elaborate and costly danced rituals, demanding expensive costumes, the maintenance of large companies of dancers and musicians, all of which were paid out of the public funds.'[6] Here, again, we are reminded of Amos, with his denunciation of the feasting and revelling, and all the noise of the viols and the extravagance of his day.[7] It was the ills of the times and all the social evils that were flowing from these sources which led these prophets, in Israel and in China, to demand their complete elimination, as a surgeon may amputate a limb under certain circumstances.[8]

For all classes Mo-tzŭ advocated hard and unremitting toil. From early morn until late at night the rulers and minor officials should devote themselves to their duties, farmers should work on the land and the women at their home industries.[9] All needless waste in clothing or in houses or equipment should be ruthlessly

[1] *Mo-tzŭ* xxv (Mei, p. 125; Forke, p. 300; Tomkinson, pp. 76 f.).
[2] *Ibid.* (Mei, p. 134; Forke, p. 312; Tomkinson, p. 83).
[3] *Mo-tzŭ* xxxii (Mei, pp. 175 ff.; Forke, pp. 364 ff.; Tomkinson, pp. 145 ff.).
[4] *Analects* VIII, viii. 3.
[5] *Hirth Anniversary Volume*, 1923, p. 617.
[6] *Three Ways of Thought in Ancient China*, p. 169.
[7] Amos v. 23.
[8] W. Corswant (*R.Th.Ph.*, N.S. xxxiv, 1946, p. 105) says: 'Déclarer que Mê Ti était parfaitement insensible à l'art, c'est aller au delà de sa pensée. Les circonstances seules l'obligent à faire passer l'utile avant l'agréable et le beau.'
[9] *Mo-tzŭ* xxxii (Mei, p. 179; Forke, p. 370; Tomkinson, p. 159).

cut out. 'What is the purpose of clothes?' he asked. 'In winter to keep out the cold, in summer to keep out the heat. The test of good clothing is therefore whether it adds warmth in winter and coolness in the summer. What is merely decorative but does not so add should be cut out.'[1]

His appeal is constantly to 'profit', which Mencius so sharply condemned. But this is linked with his demand for universal love.[2] And for this he was sternly condemned by Mencius, who believed that his principles were as dangerous as those of the pure egoist Yang Chu.[3] In the eyes of Mencius, unless these two extremes were equally rejected the foundations of civilization were threatened. Confucius had advocated love for men, but a carefully regulated love, tempered by propriety, and cherished only in appropriate and decreasing measure through the various relationships in which a man stood.[4] Mo-tzŭ, on the other hand, advocated the abolition of all distinctions and the equal love of all men,[5] and exemplified such a love in his own life. From all he called for self-sacrificing service, and he himself gave it in unstinting measure. For if Mo-tzŭ was a prophet, he was more than a prophet. Not by word alone, but by unresting example and by tireless service he sought to give effect to the reforms he believed to be so urgently needed.

[1] *Mo-tzŭ* xx (Mei, p. 117; Forke, p. 289; Tomkinson, p. 71).

[2] F. Geisser, *Mo Ti*, 1947, pp. 10 ff., reviews the preparations for Mo-tzŭ's views on this subject in the teaching of his predecessors.   [3] *Mencius* III Part 2, ix. 9.

[4] In *Analects* XII, xxii Legge translates a saying of Confucius as defining benevolence—*jên*, which Legge elsewhere renders by *perfect virtue*—with the words 'It is to love all men.' It is to be observed, however, that the crucial word *all* does not stand in the Chinese text. In the *Doctrine of the Mean* xx. 5 we probably have a reliable expression of the teaching of Confucius that love was to be carefully regulated by the rules of propriety. That this is how Mo-tzŭ understood the teaching of Confucius is clear from *Mo-tzŭ* xxxix: 'The Confucianist says, "Love among relations should depend on the degree of kinship, and the honour due to the worthy should be graded"' (Mei, p. 200; Forke, p. 395; Tomkinson, p. 159). Similarly Mencius, who so strongly objected to Mo-tzŭ's teaching of universal love, certainly did not understand Confucius to have given similar teaching. He says 'Mo's principle is "to love all equally", which does not acknowledge the peculiar affection due to a father. But to acknowledge neither King nor father is to be in the state of a beast' (*Mencius* III Part 2, ix. 9).

[5] Cf. *Mo-tzŭ* xiv-xvi (Mei, pp. 78 ff.; Forke, pp. 240 ff.; Tomkinson, pp. 49 ff.).

Nevertheless, both by his contemporaries and by modern writers he has been represented as a utilitarian because of his emphasizing of the profit that would accrue to men from the application of his principles.[1] Universal love would bring the universal profit of men, he believed, and again and again he sought to show how selfishness and war brought poverty and misery, whereas if everyone sought to give instead of to get, to serve instead of to use, all would be happier and richer. It has therefore seemed to some that his love rested on selfishness, and was rooted in its antithesis. This, I am persuaded, is not fair to Mo-tzŭ. Much Christian preaching has emphasized the peace and poise of spirit offered to men, and the hope of immortal bliss hereafter. Yet the Christian call is to a life of self-identification with Christ and of service to God and men. Mo-tzŭ's call was to service, and though he emphasized the profit that would follow if his principles were universally followed, this was represented as the consequence rather than the motive of its acceptance. Mo-tzŭ himself got no profit, but was prepared to wear himself out, as his opponents acknowledged, without the slightest hope of gain, and many of his followers followed him in this. Nowhere did he offer immediate profits to the individuals who accepted his call, and there was actually far less appeal to individual selfishness than in much Christian preaching. All that Mo-tzŭ said was that when all men accepted his teaching all would profit,[2] but it was to profit others rather than to profit self that he summoned men.[3]

[1] So *Hsün-tzŭ* xxi. 5 (cf. H. Dubs, *The Works of Hsüntze*, 1928, p. 264); F. E. A. Krause, *Ju-Tao-Fo*, 1924, p. 89; E. R. Hughes, *Chinese Philosophy in Classical Times*, 1942, p. 45. Mo-tzŭ has been called a socialist, a pacifist, a utilitarian, and a Puritan. He has been described as an anticipator of Rousseau, of John Stuart Mill, and of Aristotle, and has been declared a moral and political teacher superior to any of the Greeks (for references cf. *Submission in Suffering*, p. 113).

[2] Cf. Liang Ch'i Ch'ao, *History of Chinese Political Thought*, 1930, p. 102: 'Motze's theory does not consider the individual at all. According to him nothing is profitable unless it profits the whole of mankind. To secure this mutual profit it is necessary that all individuals should sacrifice their personal profits.'

[3] It has been noted above that Mencius strongly repudiated the very word *profit*. He rejected the idea that men should be dissuaded from war on the ground that it was unprofitable (*Mencius* VI Part 2, iv. 5), and said that this appeal could only lead to the mad rush for profit on the part of all classes of society. Here, as so often,

To this, however, we shall have to return. For the moment it may suffice to cite one passage, in which he observed that the man who accepted his principles would say 'I have heard that he who would be great amongst men should be for his friend as for himself, for his friend's parents as for his own, and only so can he become great amongst men.' The consequence of this, said Mo-tzŭ, would be that 'if he sees his friend in hunger, he will feed him; if he sees him cold, he will clothe him; if he finds him sick, he will minister to him; if dead, he will bury him. Such is the language, and such the conduct of the advocate of universality.'[1] Here is no appeal to selfishness, but only to service, and in the light of the oft-repeated teaching of Mo-tzŭ elsewhere it is clear that to the word 'friend' in this passage he would give as wide a connotation as Jesus did to the term 'neighbour' in the parable of the Good Samaritan.[2]

Between the followers of Confucius on the one hand and Mo-tzŭ and his followers on the other, there was mutual criticism and opposition, and that there were differences between them is not to be gainsaid. Yet it is possible to recognize truly prophetic qualities on both sides, and to appreciate how much is common in their concern for the condition of society in their day and in their eagerness to change that condition. All deplored the decay of society in their day and the naked selfishness that reigned. All deplored oppressive and unprincipled government, and desired to see the principles of justice[3] and benevolence put into practice.

it is important to penetrate beneath words to thought. By profit Mencius meant selfish profit, whereas Mo-tzŭ meant the general well-being. The profit that Mencius rejected was not the profit that Mo-tzŭ preached. Cf. Fung Yu-lan, *The Spirit of Chinese Philosophy*, E.Tr. by E. R. Hughes, 1947, p. 15. But that Mencius believed that virtue was profitable in a proper sense is clear from the already cited passage, in which he says that if there were a ruler who did not delight in killing men, all the people in the empire would flock to him. When Mo-tzŭ emphasized the profit that universal love would bring, it was not the profit for self, but the profit for others and for the community.

[1] *Mo-tzŭ* xvi (Mei, p. 90; Forke, p. 256; Tomkinson, p. 55).

[2] Luke x. 29 ff.

[3] A. Lods, *The Prophets and the Rise of Judaism*, E.Tr., p. 75, says: 'The originality of the great prophets in this connection consists in their declaring that divine

They differed in the degree of their interest in the common man, and Confucius's propriety was far from the abandon in service which Mo-tzŭ preached and practised. Their idiom is often very different from the idiom of our day, and is less familiar to us than the idiom of the Old Testament prophets—though that, too, is often very different from that of our day. We have been brought up with the Bible, and have a measure of familiarity with the life and conditions of ancient Israel that is wanting where the conditions of ancient China are concerned. Given the effort to understand, and to see men through the eyes of their own contemporaries and in the setting of their own times, we may see in these great men of China figures of prophetic stature, social reformers who by activity comparable with that of the prophets, and not as academicians, sought to do away with the evils of society, and to do this by changing men. All were concerned first and foremost with the spirit of men, as the prophets of Israel were. Jeremiah looked forward, in what is the most familiar word that he uttered,[1] to the time when the law of God should be inscribed not on tables of stone but on the hearts of men, when their obedience should not be to an external law that was imposed on them, but to the law that had become part of their own being. The prophets of China no less than of Israel sought to write the good law on the hearts of men.

justice is absolute, strictly impartial, unequivocal, and without reservation; Jahweh is above caprice as he is above self-interest; neither offerings nor a ritual more or less magical can influence him.' All this would have been accepted by Confucius, Mencius and Mo-tzŭ, with the substitution of *Heaven* for *Jahweh*.

[1] Jer. xxxi. 31 ff.

IV

The Prophet and the Golden Age

THE prophet always speaks primarily to his own generation. The great pre-exilic prophets of Israel uttered a message which was predominantly one of warning and rebuke. The same is true of the three Chinese Sages whom we are bringing into comparison with them. All were concerned for the state of contemporary society and sought to combat the evils they perceived and to rectify the life of the state. Too often in the study of the Israelite prophets all beside this is ignored. In the first lecture of this series I rejected the view that they were not foretellers, but only forthtellers. What I have in mind at the moment, however, is not foretelling in general. Most of the predictions of the prophets had to do with the immediate or measurable future, the future that should arise out of the present. Within the prophetic books of the Old Testament we find a number of passages which are concerned with the more distant future, or future which is not connected by any sequence of events with the speaker's own day. It lies on the far horizons of time, and is presented as a distant hope. For this remote future is always presented in roseate terms, and may be broadly described as a Golden Age.

Many scholars have denied—and still deny—these passages to the prophets in whose books they stand. They would still be evidence of an important hope which was cherished in Israel, even though they were later additions to the prophetic books. But there is a mood of greater caution today in regard to these passages, and a less hasty rejection of them as spurious.[1] The well-known passage about beating swords into ploughshares, which stands in both

---

[1] On the antiquity of this idea in Israel, cf. A. Lods, *The Prophets and the Rise of Judaism*, E.Tr., pp. 70 f.

Isaiah and Micah,[1] finds defenders for its Isaianic authorship,[2] or for the authorship of Micah,[3] and even for an earlier authorship.[4] I think it is impossible to be confident of its authorship by either of them, though the fact that it is independently ascribed to two contemporary prophets adds to the probability that its age may be correctly preserved. The passages in Isaiah ix[5] and xi,[6] which are commonly characterized as Messianic, find a large number of scholars to defend their Isaianic authorship.[7] To examine the question of their authorship here is quite impossible, and I do not wish to prejudge any question.[8] The number and distribution of such passages, however, is evidence that the broad hope which they embody, though presented in a variety of differing forms, was an important element of prophetic teaching. The Golden Age lay in the future. To apocalyptists, like the author of the book of Daniel, it lay just round the corner, when the intervention of God to wind up the ordinary process of history and to establish the enduring kingdom was expected; but most of these passages elsewhere are

---

[1] Isa. ii. 2 ff., Mic. iv. 1 ff.

[2] So, e.g., B. Duhm, *Das Buch Jesaia*, 2nd ed., 1902, p. 14; H. Schmidt, *Die grossen Propheten*, 2nd ed., 1923, p. 112 n.; J. Fischer, *Das Buch Isaias*, i, 1937, p. 36; E. J. Kissane, *The Book of Isaiah*, i, 1941, p. 22; L. Dennefeld, *Les grands prophètes*, 1946, p. 28 a.

[3] So, e.g., C. Cornill, *Introduction to the Canonical Books of the Old Testament*, E.Tr. by G. H. Box, 1907, pp. 269 f.; A. van Hoonacker, *Les douze Petits Prophètes*, 1908, p. 381; S. Bullough, *Obadiah, Micah, Zephaniah, Haggai and Micah*, 1953, p. 77.

[4] So, e.g., A. Condamin, *Le livre d'Isaïe*, 1905, pp. 20 ff.; G. H. Box, *The Book of Isaiah*, 1916, p. 31; F. Feldmann, *Das Buch Isaias*, i, 1925, p. 25.

[5] Isa. ix. 2 ff. (Heb. 1 ff.).

[6] Isa. xi. 1 ff.

[7] So, e.g., Duhm, *op. cit.*, pp. 62 f., 77; Condamin, *op. cit.*, pp. 77, 96; Cornill, *op. cit.*, p. 271; Box, *op. cit.*, pp. 54 f., 67 f.; Schmidt, *op. cit.*, pp. 114 ff.; Feldmann, *op. cit.*, pp. 122 ff., 161; Fischer, *op. cit.*, pp. 83 f., 101; Kissane, *op. cit.*, pp. 105, 133; Dennefeld, *op. cit.*, pp. 50 b, 58 b. O. Eissfeldt (*Einleitung in das Alte Testament*, 1934, pp. 357 ff.) holds the former passage to be probably Isaianic and the latter probably not, and so Oesterley and Robinson (*Introduction to the Books of the Old Testament*, 1934, pp. 245 f.).

[8] Cf. J. Bright, *The Kingdom of God*, 1953, p. 83 n.: 'While, of course, the genuineness of such passages cannot be proved mathematically, the arguments for relegating them to a later era are more than dubious. They may safely be regarded as expressions of the prophetic mind of the late eighth and early seventh centuries.'

introduced vaguely by some such phrase as 'in the latter end of the days'.[1]

In some respects the prophets sometimes idealized the Mosaic age. Jeremiah could refer to it as the bridal days of the nation, marked by devotion to God,[2] though he could elsewhere speak of the stubbornness that had characterized Israel from the day when she came out of Egypt.[3] Amos could appeal to the practice of the wilderness days as an ideal to be copied.[4] But the Mosaic age was not thought of as the Golden Age representing a glory that was never to be recaptured. It could bring inspiration just because there was a grander hope before men. Had it been thought of merely as a lost glory that was gone for ever, followed by a defection that was final, there would have been little point in the prophetic zeal to reform society, and to recall men to the obedience of former days.

That the prophets were not without any hope for the future is clear from their thought of the Remnant.[5] This thought is found

[1] This phrase is usually associated with Hebrew eschatology. As to how far it is legitimate to speak of eschatology in the prophets, cf. J. Lindblom, in *Studia Theologica*, VI. ii, 1953, pp. 79 ff., and Th. C. Vriezen, in *Supplements to V.T.*, i: *Congress Volume*, 1953, pp. 199 ff.

[2] Jer. ii. 2.

[3] Jer. vii. 24 ff.

[4] Amos v. 25. This verse is taken by most scholars to imply that in the view of Amos no sacrifices were offered in the wilderness days. As this is without historical foundation, and as the traditions at variance with this view are older than the time of Amos, it is likely that if he wished to challenge them he would have done so directly, and not by a rhetorical question which implied that everyone knew the truth. V. Maag (*Text, Wortschatz und Begriffswelt des Buches Amos*, 1951, pp. 221 ff.) thinks Amos relies on a lost variant historical source, though he agrees that such a source was without foundation in fact. W. O. E. Oesterley (*Sacrifices in Ancient Israel*, 1937, p. 195) and H. Junker (*Theologie und Glaube*, 1935, pp. 686 ff.) hold that the answer expected by the text was 'Yes'. I have elsewhere (*B.J.R.L.*, xxix, 1945–6, p. 342 n.) indicated my acceptance of the view of D. B. Macdonald (*J.B.L.*, xviii, 1899, pp. 214 f.), that the text really means 'Was it only flesh-sacrifices and meal-offerings that ye brought me in the wilderness?' where the expected answer is 'We brought more than this; we brought true worship of heart and righteousness.' But however the verse is interpreted, it implies an appeal to the standards of the wilderness days.

[5] Cf. R. de Vaux, *R.B.*, xlii, 1933, pp. 526 ff.; H. Dittmann, *T.S.K.*, lxxxvii, 1914, pp. 603 ff.; E. W. Heaton, *J.T.S.*, N.S. iii, 1952, pp. 27 ff.; J. Bright, *op.*

in varying forms throughout the Bible, but here it is only of the prophets that we can think. The idea of the Remnant is especially associated with Isaiah, whose son was symbolically named Shear Jashub.[1] This name means 'A remnant shall return', or 'shall repent'. It embodies both judgement and hope. Sometimes only the hope is read into it, and sometimes only the judgement. It is clear that Isaiah meant 'Only a remnant',[2] and to this extent there was judgement involved; nevertheless, if even a remnant survived the judgement, there was hope involved. Isaiah thought of a remnant that should justify its survival by the loyalty it would bring to God, as he makes plain when he says that the spared remnant would stay themselves upon God.[3] He thought of a remnant that should be spared for blessing, that would take root downwards and bear fruit upward,[4] unto whom Yahweh of hosts would be a crown of glory.[5] Whether the disputed passages to which I have referred are by Isaiah or not, therefore, they are not unrelated to this element of his thought.

Even before Isaiah, Amos had spoken of a remnant that should be spared, as a few scraps of an animal might be rescued from the mouth of a lion.[6] He could think of this remnant as spared, not for its own loyalty or worth, but failing to justify its survival by unwillingness still to return in loyalty to God,[7] though he could equally appeal to men to hate evil and to love good, and to establish justice, so that perchance God might spare them.[8] Similarly

---

cit., pp. 71 ff.; also my *Biblical Doctrine of Election*, 1950, pp. 71 ff. The most extended study of the Remnant is S. Garofalo, *La nozione profetica del 'Resto d'Israele'*, 1942.

[1] Isa. vii. 3. [2] Isa. x. 22.

[3] Isa. x. 20. [4] Isa. xxxvii. 31.

[5] Isa. xxviii. 5. In view of what will be said below of the character of the Golden Age in prophetic thought, it may be noted that the following verse speaks of the spirit of justice which shall be found in the courts.

[6] Amos iii. 12. [7] Amos iv. 11.

[8] Amos v. 15. S. R. Driver (*The Books of Joel and Amos*, 2nd ed., edited by H. C. O. Lanchester, p. 186) says 'The prophet can hardly be thinking of the remnant to which Joseph had been already reduced. . . . No doubt he has mentally in view the "remnant", to which he sees that before long it will have been actually reduced.'

Zephaniah could appeal to men to do the will of God and to seek righteousness, so that perchance they might be spared in the day of wrath.[1] In all these cases, whether the remnant was spared for its loyalty or not, it was conceived of as the heir of the Covenant, to carry to a future generation the faith so imperfectly apprehended in the prophets' own days. Prophets who proclaimed this could not have been wholly without hope for the future. The present was black and the immediate future grave. But beyond it lay a hope which the present did not inspire.

When we look at the passages which tell of the Golden Age on the horizons of time, we find that the element of universality belongs to it. It is perceived that one people cannot know ideal conditions while it is set in the midst of a world that does not share them. It must be remembered that the very situation of Israel helped to point this truth. Set in a land that was so often the cockpit of the great powers, between the rival empires that successively sought dominion throughout much or the whole of the ancient Near East, it was impossible to anticipate the Golden Age for Israel, while the neighbouring peoples continued to contend for power. Enduring peace throughout the world was an essential element of the age to which the prophets in these passages looked forward. Sometimes the economic consequences of enduring peace and security were described,[2] and sometimes the peace was thought of as extending to the animal creation, when the very natures of beasts would be transformed to match the changed character of men.[3]

Nowhere is it supposed that this ideal future would develop of itself out of the present, or by human efforts to reach understanding, or by a steady increase of man's wisdom. Whether the term is

---

[1] Zeph. ii. 3.   [2] Mic. iv. 4; cf. Isa. lxvi. 22 ff.

[3] Isa. xi. 6 ff. Most commentators hold that the prophet thinks of the future Golden Age in terms of a restored Paradise. But J. Steinmann, Le prophète Isaïe, 1950, pp. 169 f., holds that the images are used metaphorically for men, just as the vine in Isa. v. 1 ff. stands for men. He says: 'Le loup, la panthère, le lion, l'ourse, le cobra et la vipère sont les images des magistrats corrompus, des guerriers sans pitié, des propriétaires forciers qui pressuraient les pauvres paysans et les miséreux.' For the general conception of the passage cf. Isa. lxv. 25.

used or not, it was always thought of as fundamentally a Kingdom of God, in which God's will would be universally done. It would be a kingdom in which righteousness would prevail,[1] for the Hebrew prophets were too realistic to expect the fruits of peace from the tree of unrighteousness. But righteousness was to be equated with the doing of God's will, and men who did not know God or understand His law could not stumble into the way of His will. Hence the *sine qua non* for the Golden Age was the universal sway of one whose rule would be the expression of God's will, in a world where all men sought to learn and to obey that will. It was not mere Jewish nationalism or megalomania which caused the prophets to think of the Golden Age in these terms. If the passages did indeed come from the prophets to whom they are ascribed, their other oracles sufficiently show that they were not rabid nationalists and megalomaniacs. They were rather men who saw that unity and universality were not sufficient to ensure ideal conditions, but that the quality that belonged to the unity and universality was even more important, and who recognized that the will of God was the only basis for the Golden Age. They were sure that to Israel the will of God had been revealed, and it was for this reason and this alone that the leadership in that age was expected to belong to Israel and her king. It was not because Israel was so much better than others in their eyes. The prophets constantly castigated the Israel that was. But they were sure that to Israel had been entrusted a heritage of supreme value, and that it was as the custodian of that heritage, rather than in virtue of her own nobility, that she was destined to play so high a part in the Kingdom of God.

Of this picture not all of the elements are found in any one of the passages which speak of this hope. Some emphasize the role of the Davidic leader and some do not mention him. For each of these prophets gave his own individual description of the glory to which they all looked forward. But all thought of a universal and enduring glory, which should be the expression of the rule of God amongst men.

[1] Isa. ix. 7 (Heb. 6), xi. 4 f., Jer. xxiii. 5 f.

It is both impossible and unnecessary for us here to examine in detail all of the passages in the prophets relating to these hopes, but brief reference may be made to a few of the more familiar amongst them. In the oft-cited passage about beating swords into ploughshares, this is presented as the consequence of the resort of men to God to learn his will.[1] It is when all nations stream to the house of the God of Jacob, to learn his ways, and when He judges between the nations and reproves those that deserve reproof, that they beat their swords into ploughshares and learn war no more. In the form which this oracle has in the book of Micah there is added a verse which notes the economic consequences of this universal acceptance of the will of God, by saying that every man would sit under his own vine or fig-tree, with none to make him afraid.[2]

In the passage in the book of Isaiah which tells of the birth of the hoped-for Davidic leader, it is emphasized that his rule would be upheld with judgement and righteousness, and that it would therefore be enduring and would be marked by unbroken peace.[3] Two chapters later we read of the shoot from the stock of Jesse, on whom the spirit of the Lord would rest, and who should therefore have wisdom to rule in righteousness and strength.[4] The bliss of that age is here represented as reflected in the animal world, so that the wolf should dwell with the lamb, and the leopard with the kid.[5] The passage closes with a verse which is often thought to be originally independent of it, but which fits well into its thought.[6] It declares that the earth shall be full of the knowledge of the Lord, as the waters cover the sea.[7] The will of God is the

---

[1] Isa. ii. 3 f. Cf. J. Bright, *The Kingdom of God*, 1953, p. 95: 'A moral world order is inconceivable and impossible save in submission to the righteous rule of God.'

[2] Mic. iv. 4.   [3] Isa. ix. 6 f. (Heb. 5 f.).
[4] Isa. xi. 1 ff.   [5] Isa. xi. 6 f.; cf. above, p. 78 n.
[6] Cf. what I have written in *The Missionary Message of the Old Testament*, 1945, p. 43: 'Whether it was the compiler of the book of Isaiah, or the spokesman of the oracle, that brought all this together, the connexion was wisely made. For in the wholeness of its picture we again see a world united and at peace, with the spirit of concord spreading even to the lower creation, and all resting on a universal faith.'   [7] Isa. xi. 9; cf. Hab. ii. 14.

only basis offered to men as the foundation of the Golden Age.

Jeremiah speaks of a branch of David, through whom Israel should be saved and given security.[1] Here there is no mention of the universality of his sway, but it is said that he should administer justice in the land, and that the king should be so closely associated with God that his name would be called Yahweh our Righteousness.[2] In another passage Jeremiah speaks of the New Covenant which God would make with Israel, when His law would be written on men's hearts and their iniquity be remembered no more.[3] There is here no mention of the Davidic leader, no mention of universality, no mention of peace or the outer conditions of life. Yet it is clear that there is the thought of obedience to the will of God as complete within the life of the nation. All would know God, and since iniquity would be forgotten, and iniquity is whatever is alien to the will of God, the will of God would prevail unchallenged throughout the land.

The great prophet of the exile, whom we call Deutero-Isaiah, in his picture of the Golden Age does not mention the Davidic leader, but speaks of the time when the judgement of God should go forth to all the world, and when the isles should wait for Him, when the heavens and the earth should vanish but an age of everlasting righteousness should begin.[4] To him, as to all the prophets, the only true basis of unity was in the will of God, and only a world that acknowledged His sway could find true well-being. 'Look unto me, and be ye saved, all the ends of the earth,' he

---

[1] Jer. xxiii. 5 f. P. Volz (Der Prophet Jeremia, 2nd ed., 1928, pp. 232f.) doubts the Jeremianic authorship of this passage, and so some other scholars. A. S. Peake Jeremiah, i, p. 260) and W. Rudolph (Jeremia, 1947, pp. 125 ff.) defend its genuineness.

[2] Yahweh Ṣidhḳēnû. There is here perhaps some play on the name of the reigning King Zedekiah, i.e. Ṣidhḳîyāhû, which means Yahweh is my Righteousness. On this whole passage cf. J. Skinner, Prophecy and Religion, 1922, pp. 310 ff.

[3] Jer. xxxi. 31 ff. The Jeremianic authorship of this passage has been challenged by many scholars, but on grounds which to others are not convincing. Cf. L. E. Binns, The Book of the Prophet Jeremiah, 1919, pp. 241 ff., and especially the careful discussion in J. Skinner, Prophecy and Religion, pp. 320 ff.

[4] Isa. li. 4 ff.

cries elsewhere, 'for I am God, and there is no other.'[1] Instead of
the Davidic Messiah he gives us the figure of the Servant of Yahweh,[2] whose mission was to bring forth judgement in faithfulness,
until he had established it in all the earth.[3] Too small a thing was it
for the Servant to restore the tribes of Jacob; his mission was to be
the light of the nations, and to carry the salvation of God to the
ends of the earth.[4]

Into this mission the whole nation was called to enter. I cannot
here discuss the identification of the Servant, which I have more
than once discussed elsewhere.[5] The simple identification of the
Servant with Israel does not seem to me satisfactory, while the
complete separation of the Servant and Israel seems no more so.
I think the Servant is a concept that oscillates between the nation
and an individual who should in himself carry its mission to its
supreme point, but who in doing so should call the whole nation
to share that mission. We find outside the Servant Songs Israel
called the servant,[6] and declared to be the light of the nations,[7]
as the Servant is within the Songs,[8] and to Israel it is said 'Ye are
my witnesses, and my servant, whom I have chosen.'[9] The
Golden Age could not come until all the world was brought under
the rule of God, but Israel was called to spread the light and not
merely to wait passively until the Kingdom should come.

In the closing chapters of the book of Isaiah, which are commonly attributed to disciples of Deutero-Isaiah of a later date, we
find a reference to the new heaven and new earth,[10] of which
Deutero-Isaiah had given more than a hint.[11] Human life should be

---

[1] Isa. xlv. 22. R. Levy (*Deutero-Isaiah*, 1925, p. 195) says this is 'the grandest
verse in the prophet's scroll'.

[2] This figure is presented in the Servant Songs, which are most commonly de-
limited as Isa. xlii. 1–4, xlix. 1–6, l. 4–9, lii. 13–liii. 12. For some other delimita-
tions cf. my *Servant of the Lord*, 1952, p. 6 n.

[3] Isa. xlii. 3 f.   [4] Isa. xlix. 6.

[5] Cf. *Israel's Mission to the World*, 1939, pp. 10 ff.; *The Missionary Message of
the Old Testament*, pp. 51 ff.; *The Biblical Doctrine of Election*, 1950, pp. 111 ff.;
and, especially, *The Servant of the Lord*, 1952, pp. 3 ff.

[6] Cf. Isa. xli. 8 f., xliv. 1.   [7] Isa. xlii. 6.

[8] Isa. xlix. 6.   [9] Isa. xliii. 10.

[10] Isa. lxv. 17.   [11] Isa. li. 4 ff.

preternaturally extended, and be spared its present vicissitudes, and bliss should be everlasting.[1] But this bliss, as another passage tells us, could be attained when all flesh should come to worship Yahweh.[2] As always, the essence of the Golden Age was to be found in a spiritual change in men, and in the acceptance of the rule of God.

This whole conception is thus one which is found widely in the prophets, with important common features through all its diversity of expression. It is not confined to the prophets, indeed, but may be found also in some of the psalms. These lie beyond our present range, though we may perhaps spare a moment to look at one of them, which ties particularly closely with this hope. This is Psalm lxxii, which is a prayer for the king. It prays that his dominion might be from sea to sea, from the River to the ends of the earth, and that his foes might be crushed beneath him.[3] But here, as elsewhere, his dominion is not just ruthless suppression, but deeply based on righteousness. The poor and needy should find in him a defender, and his rule to all generations is asked.[4] That this psalm has in mind the Davidic king, depicted in some of the passages in Isaiah, is highly probable, and there is every probability that it comes from the pre-exilic age. It may have been used in the ritual of that age in connection with the reigning king, before whose eyes was set the ideal king of the future. The hope of the Golden Age was also an inspiration. It could only be the gift of God to men, and it would not come of itself, or be brought about by merely human activity. Yet all who in their station brought to God their loyalty and devotion, and lived by the principles that would be universal in that Age, were already the children of that Age. They might be righteous rulers, witnesses of their faith, or members of the Remnant who should carry forward the heritage of Israel to the glorious time that was coming. While the Kingdom of God was never connected causally with the

---

[1] Isa. lxv. 20 ff. [2] Isa. lxvi. 22 f. [3] Psa. lxxii. 8 f.
[4] Psa. lxxii. 12 ff., 17. R. V. renders 'His name shall endure for ever; His name shall be continued as long as the sun.' The verbs are more probably to be read as jussives: 'May his name be for ever....' So R.S.V.

events of their own day, as the ills which they predicted would spring from the policies and iniquities of their time, the message of the far-off glories was not unrelated to the message which the prophets delivered in their other utterances. All their work was designed to call men to utter loyalty and obedience to God, and the pictures of the age of bliss when that obedience would be universal could only reinforce their call, by declaring the supreme worth-whileness of the life to which they summoned men.

When we turn from this to Confucius and Mencius we are in another world, and it would be easy to dismiss them as not able to be brought into anything more than a complete contrast to the prophets of Israel in relation to the hope of the Golden Age. The prophets conceived of the Golden Age as the universal rule of God, and especially through His chosen king. Their hope was essentially based on religion, and rested on obedience to the law of God. We shall have to consider the religious element in the prophets and in the Chinese Sages later, and we may therefore leave this aside for the present. What we have rather to ask here is whether Confucius and Mencius set before men any hope of a Golden Age as an inspiration to the acceptance of their teachings, and how they conceived of that age.

The selfish egoist Yang Chu,[1] whom Legge calls 'about "the least erected spirit" who ever professed to reason concerning the life and duties of man',[2] could have no conception of a Golden Age. His principle, as Mencius declared, was 'Each one for himself',[3] and he went on to add 'Though he might have benefited the whole empire by plucking out a single hair, he would not have done it.'[4] Such a man was no child of a Golden Age, and could not even understand it.[5] The author of the *Tao Tê Ching*

---

[1] On Yang Chu cf. *Lieh-tzǔ* vii (Wieger, *Taoïsme*, ii, pp. 172 ff., Legge, *The Chinese Classics*, ii, 2nd ed., pp. 93 ff., Wilhelm, *Liä Dsi*, pp. 76 ff., or A. Forke, *Yang Chu's Garden of Pleasure*, 1912, pp. 54 ff.).

[2] *Op. cit.*, p. 92.   [3] *Mencius* VII Part I, xxvi. 1.

[4] *Ibid.* Cf. *Lieh-tzǔ* vii (Wieger, *op. cit.*, pp. 172 f., Legge, *op. cit.*, pp. 95 f.).

[5] It is from *Lieh-tzǔ* that we have the fullest and the grossest accounts of the selfish hedonism of Yang Chu. Fung Yu-lan (*History of Chinese Philosophy*, i, pp. 133 ff.) thinks Yang Chu's views are presented in distorted form by *Lieh-tzǔ*.

could hold before men the individual ideal of a life which was indifferent to all but itself,[1] though more worthy than the grossness of Yang Chu. But no hope of anything worthy to be called a Golden Age could be reached along this line. But Confucius and Mencius with their interest in men and their purpose to reform the life of their day were not so shut out from the possibility of a vision of a better day.

To Confucius the past glories of Yao and Shun were an inspiration, a time to be looked back upon with wistfulness from the dark days in which he lived.[2] Then the kingdom had a wise and

While it may well be true that there is some exaggeration, there seems little reason to doubt that he was fundamentally egoistic, since this accords with the references to him elsewhere. Wilhelm (*A Short History of Chinese Civilization*, E.Tr., p. 148) says: 'The doctrines of Yang Chu therein (i.e. in *Lieh-tzŭ*) described tally remarkably well with those with which his great adversary, Mencius, upbraids him.' For an account of Yang Chu cf. Forke, *Geschichte der alten chinesischen Philosophie*, pp. 356 ff. F. E. A. Krause (*Ju-Tao-Fo*, 1924, p. 87) says: 'Er ist Sensualist und Epikureer, sein System ein egoistischer Individualismus, der theoretischen Pessimismus und praktische Eudaimonologie vereinigt.'

[1] The question of the authorship and date of the *Tao Tê Ching* lie far outside my subject here. The book is traditionally ascribed to an older contemporary of Confucius, but this tradition is widely rejected today, and the book is ascribed to a much later author, who is identified by some, but treated as unknown by others. Cf. *Submission in Suffering*, p. 108 n. H. Maspero (*Le Taoïsme*, 1950, p. 229) says: 'Lao-tseu n'est qu'un nom, et le petit traité qui est attribué tantôt à lui, tantôt au mythique Empereur Jaune, le *Tao-tö-king*, date probablement du début ou du milieu du ive siècle.' In the latest publication on the book the distinguished Leiden professor, J. J. L. Duyvendak, says he finds it impossible to place the book earlier than about 300 B.C. (*Tao Te Ching*, 1954, p. 7). Of the *tê*, or virtue, of this book he says: 'It is completely amoral and it is diametrically opposed to what others regard as virtue' (p. 11). He finds a polemic against the Confucian school's effort to transform the *tao*, or *way*, into an ethical concept, and continues: 'The Taoist Saint is the very opposite of the Confucian one, who is concerned about the reform of the world through education in moral virtues. The Taoist behaves like a divine fool, an arch-individualist, who keeps aloof from the world and its activities, and who, in a mystical experience, attains directly the unity with the Way' (p. 12).

[2] Cf. *Analects* VIII, xix f. Cf. also Mo-tzŭ's high regard for these ancient Kings (*Mo-tzŭ* xxi, Mei, pp. 120 ff., Forke, pp. 292 ff., Tomkinson, pp. 73 ff.). With this contrast Yang Chu's scorn for Yao and Shun (*Lieh-tzŭ* vii, Wieger, *op. cit.*, pp. 172 ff., Legge, *op. cit.*, pp. 96 f.). Yao and Shun are regarded as legendary, unhistorical characters (so Wilhelm, *Confucius and Confucianism*, p. 100 n.), but this is immaterial for our purpose, since they stood for an ideal which was set before men.

benevolent government which made it in retrospect seem a Golden Age. Reference has already been made to a passage in the Shu Ching, which speaks of Wu, the overthrower of the tyrant Chou.[1] In that passage Wu says that rulers were ordained of God to help Him in His purposes towards men and to preserve the peace of the state.[2] The role here assigned to the king has points of comparison with the role of the Davidic king in the Israelite pictures of the Golden Age, and perhaps with the role that was set before the contemporary king in the ritual by the recital of such a psalm as Psalm lxxii.

Confucius presents no sure promise of a like age in the future, such as the Israelite prophets presented in the passages to which we have referred, and in others that might be added to them. Yet he must have cherished the vision of such an age, though his hope of it was so much fainter. The man who believed that if he were put in charge of the state and given three years of opportunity he could bring about the perfection of the state[3] must have had the vision of a perfect state. His conception of the way in which it might be brought about was very different from that of the prophets. He thought it might be attained by purely human effort, and be evolved from the chaos of his own day in a very short time by human wisdom. This is not intended to imply that he left the divine will out of account. He believed that the mandate of Heaven rested upon him.[4] But so the prophets of Israel believed that the mandate of Heaven rested on them. Yet none of them supposed that by his efforts he could bring in the Golden Age. To Confucius the task seemed a far easier one than it seemed to them.

Again, Confucius differed from the prophets in that his thought was normally limited to the Chinese empire of his day—and this was but a part of what we think of as China today. He made some references to the savage tribes beyond the borders of the empire, but he was not very concerned about them. We find nothing

---

[1] *Shu Ching* V Book 1, Part 1, 4 ff.   [2] *Shu Ching* V Book 1, Part 1, 7.
[3] *Analects* XIII, x. Cf. *Analects* XIII, xii, where it is said that if a truly royal ruler were to arise, it would take a generation before virtue (*jên*) would prevail.
[4] *Analects* IX, v.

here comparable with the universalism of the Hebrews, or comparable with the missionary purpose there set before men. To criticize Confucius for this is not really justified, however. As has been said, Israel's situation in the midst of contending empires meant that her experience told her there could be no hope for her well-being and enduring peace until the nations around her shared it. Confucius was set in a very different situation. He lived in an empire which was nominally one, but which in practice was a loose association of selfish and scheming princes. The states beyond the boundaries of the empire did not seriously affect the life of China, and it is not to be wondered at that his thought was limited to the ways in which an ideal condition might be achieved for the empire. This was his world, and he is not to be depreciated because the range of his vision was not wider.

Within that world he had a vision of perfect government, which was implicit in much of his teaching. If the government were inspired by the right principles, he believed that the ideal could become actual. And those principles were not wholly unworthy to be set beside the principles which in the prophetic visions of the Golden Age were looked for as the governing principles of the rule of the Davidic king. Confucius described those principles as righteousness, benevolence, sincerity, faithfulness. These were the things he desired to see exemplified in the government, and permeating the whole of the five relations of society. If he did not predict the Golden Age he worked for it, and he worked for it because he had beheld its glories afar off; and he perceived as clearly as any of the prophets of Israel that the fundamental condition for its realization lay in the renewal of the spirit of men.

As to the means whereby that renewal might be brought about he differed widely from the prophets. He relied far too largely on the power of example. 'If a superior love propriety' he said, 'the people will not dare not to be reverent. If he love righteousness, the people will not dare not to submit to his example. If he love good faith, the people will not dare not to be sincere. Now when these things obtain, the people from all quarters will come to him, bearing their children on their backs.'[1] Similarly in the *Chia Yü* we find Confucius credited with the saying: 'In the Way of man, government is the greatest thing. Now government means to be correct.[2] If the ruler does what is correct, then the people will follow and be correct. Whatever the ruler does, the people follow. If the ruler does not do what is correct, what do the people have to follow?'[3] This simple assumption we have found also in the teaching of Mencius, who relied no less than his Master on the power of example.[4] In the previous lecture I cited passages from Mencius which declared that if a single ruler were concerned to give his people peace and benevolent government, all the people of the empire would flock to him, and nothing could prevent him from gaining imperial sway. It is clear that to Mencius this imperial sway would bring ideal conditions for all the people.

The Commentary on the *Great Learning* is therefore true to the principles of Confucius when it declares that Yao and Shun set an example of benevolence in the government and the people followed them, while Chieh and Chou set examples of violence which were similarly followed.[5] 'On this account', continues the Commentary, 'the ruler must himself be possessed of the good qualities, and then he may require them in the people. . . . Never has there been a man who, not having reference to his own character and wishes in dealing with others,[6] was able effectually to instruct them.' And again later in the same Commentary we read 'Never has there been a case of the sovereign loving benevolence, and the people not loving righteousness.'[7]

In the text of the *Great Learning* we find it stated that these were the roots of the Golden Age of the past. 'The ancients who wished to illustrate illustrious virtue throughout the empire,

---

[1] *Analects* XIII, iv. 3.

[2] The same play on words that we have found in the Analects. Cf. above, p. 58 n.

[3] Kramers, *K'ung Tzu Chia Yü*, p. 212 (I, 12a, Sect. iv).

[4] *Mencius* IV Part 1, xx: 'Let the prince be correct, and everything will be correct.' Cf. also *Mencius* IV Part 2, v.

[5] *Great Learning*, Commentary ix. 4.

[6] I.e. without *shu*; cf. above, p. 62 n.

[7] *Great Learning*, Commentary x. 21.

first ordered well their own states. Wishing to order well their states, they first regulated their families. Wishing to regulate their families, they first cultivated their persons. Wishing to cultivate their persons, they first rectified their hearts. Wishing to rectify their hearts, they first sought to be sincere in their thoughts. Wishing to be sincere in their thoughts, they first extended to the utmost their knowledge. Such extension of knowledge lay in the investigation of things. Things being investigated, knowledge became complete. Their knowledge being complete, their thoughts were sincere. Their thoughts being sincere, their hearts were rectified. Their hearts being rectified, their persons were cultivated. Their persons being cultivated, their families were regulated. Their families being regulated, their states were rightly governed. Their states being rightly governed, the whole empire was made tranquil and happy.'[1] Since this was presented as instruction, and especially as instruction to rulers,[2] it was apparently intended to offer a prescription for the renewal of the Golden Age. It was a Golden Age that man was believed to be capable of making for himself, and it had no deeper foundation than the will of the sovereign. Nor had it the everlasting quality of the Golden Age of the Israelite prophets. It was dependent not on God, but on the king, and unless his successor shared the same spirit, its basis had gone, and with it the Golden Age must again vanish. The same easy prescription for the Golden Age is found in the *Doctrine of the Mean*: 'It is only he who is possessed of the most complete sincerity that can exist under heaven, who can give its full development to his own nature. Able to give its full development to his own nature, he can do the same to the nature of other men. Able to give its full development to the nature of other men, he can give their full development to the natures of animals and things. Able to give their full development to the natures of creatures and things, he can assist the transforming and nourishing powers of Heaven and Earth. Able to assist the transforming and nourishing powers of Heaven and Earth, he may with Heaven and

---

[1] *Great Learning*, Text 4 f.
[2] Cf. Legge, *The Chinese Classics*, i, 2nd ed., p. 29.

Earth form a ternion.'[1] This savours more of the dream of the philosopher than the vision of the prophet, and the humanism of Confucius has become empty words.

Mo-tzŭ's dominant principle of universal mutual love led him more readily to the thought of the Golden Age, when this principle should be adopted by all. He advocated an undiscriminating love of everybody, instead of the gradations of love according to the various relationships of society which Confucius inculcated. To his opponents he appeared to be undermining the very foundations of society. They were afraid that it meant that men would feel no more obligation to those who were near than to those who were far, whereas Mo-tzŭ's emphasis was rather that men should feel no less obligation to those who were far than to those who were near. He sought to scale love up to its highest level; they feared the effect might be to scale it down to its lowest. Certain it is that amongst the followers of Mo-tzŭ selfishness soon appeared, and the high level of love which he demanded was forgotten.[2] Some of his immediate disciples, however, rose to heights of self-forgetting service comparable with his own.[3] For Mo-tzŭ demanded a love for another's father equal to love for one's own, love for a friend equal to love for oneself.[4] As I said in the last lecture, this could bring little profit unless it were universalized, and in all his insistence on the profit which he believed would be

[1] *Doctrine of the Mean* xxii.

[2] Cf. *Han-Fei-tzŭ* 1 (not included in Liao's translation so far issued). The relevant passage is cited and translated by Forke, *Mê Ti*, p. 75. Cf. also *Chuang-tzŭ* xxxiii. 2 (Legge, *Sacred Books of the East*, xl, pp. 220 f., Giles, *Chuang Tzŭ*, pp. 442 f., or Wieger, *Taoïsme*, ii, pp. 500 f.).

[3] Huai-Nan-tzŭ says Mo-tzŭ had a bodyguard of 180 men, who would willingly go to death by fire or sword at his command (cf. Fung Yu-lan, *History of Chinese Philosophy*, i, p. 82), and the *Lü Shih Ch'un Ch'iu* gives an account of the heroic self-sacrifice of 183 of his followers, moved by no seeking for profit, but only by the desire to protect the oppressed (XIX, iii. Wilhelm, *Frühling und Herbst des Lü Bu We*, pp. 327 f.). To this it may be added that *Chuang-tzŭ* xxxiii. 2 associates Ch'in Hua-li, one of Mo-tzŭ's immediate disciples, with his Master's self sacrificing spirit. Cf. Wilhelm, *A Short History of Chinese Civilization*, p. 151: 'Its adherents sacrificed themselves for the world, relinquishing every comfort and every joy.'

[4] *Mo-tzŭ* xvi (Mei, pp. 89 f.; Forke, pp. 255 f., Tomkinson, pp. 54 f.).

the issue of this love, Mo-tzŭ spoke of the time when all should practise it.

Here, then, he presents a picture of the Golden Age, and in some respects it is not unworthy to be placed beside the hope and promise set before Israel by her prophets. If Mo-tzŭ insisted on the profit that would be found by all in that age, it must be remembered that the Old Testament also depicts the peace and security, and the economic bliss of the messianic age. Many of the critics of Mo-tzŭ, both in ancient and modern times, stigmatize him as a mere utilitarian who demanded love because love would pay. It would be just as easy to criticize the prophets of Israel on the ground that they believed that if men would do the will of God their well-being would be assured. They threatened disasters to a generation that disobeyed the will of God, but believed that if men would truly return to God, the disasters might be averted. There was an appeal to interest in their word as well as in Mo-tzŭ's. But there was more than this appeal in theirs, and more too in his. The prophets believed that the will of God was supremely good in itself, and that Israel owed Him obedience by all that He had done for her. So, too, Mo-tzŭ believed that the way of universal love was supremely good in itself, or he would not have pursued it independently of any profit it brought him, but rather at the cost of suffering.[1] The profit lay in the Golden Age for him, as it lay for the prophets of Israel so far as its full consummation was concerned. They believed that by immediate obedience the threatened disasters might be averted, but they did not think the full consummation could be reached by Israel alone. And until all reached it, Israel could not know its full glories. I cannot see why Mo-tzŭ should be so stigmatized because he realized that the spirit to which he called men would be incalculably beneficial to men if only all shared it.

'Suppose everybody in the world loved universally,' he said,

---

[1] Cf. *Mo-tzŭ* xlvi (Mei, pp. 213 f.; Forke, pp. 539 f.; Tomkinson, p. 124), where Wu-Ma-tzŭ reproaches Mo-tzŭ with the futility of his service for the world, and Mo-tzŭ defends the worthwhileness of his effort and intention quite independently of his success.

'loving others as themselves. Would there be anyone unfilial? When everyone regarded his father, elder brother, and emperor as himself, towards whom would they be unfilial? Would there still be anyone unaffectionate? When every one regarded his younger brother, son, and minister as himself, towards whom would they display disaffection? Therefore there would not be any unfilial feeling or disaffection. Would there be any thieves and robbers? When every one regarded other families as his own family, who would rob? When every one regarded other persons as his own person, who would steal?'[1]

In all this there is nothing ignoble. It can hardly be supposed that virtue would be more attractive if it could be guaranteed to increase the miseries of men. Should we condemn in our modern world anything which promised to eliminate the crimes of violence with which our newspapers are filled, on the ground that this was a worthless utilitarianism? Are we so in love with the fruits of selfishness that we could only approve of unselfishness provided it left those fruits unchanged? If it is true that when men truly loved one another, they would serve one another, and refrain from injuring and robbing one another, there is nothing improper in saying so. The prophets of Israel, and all social reformers everywhere, including the Confucian Sages, wished to eliminate the evils of the society of their day, and to bring about a better condition of society. Why should Mo-tzŭ alone be condemned for this, as though he were guilty of something shameful? Nowhere did he say to men 'Practice this love for what you will get out of it as individuals. Follow me and it will pay you.' He summoned men to the way of universal love because it was the good way, and its goodness would be apparent to all when all followed it.

I am aware that there may be brought against me such a passage as the following to show that Mo-tzŭ did sometimes teach 'Follow me and it will pay you.' In the first of the Synoptic chapters on the Will of Heaven he says: 'Whoso obeys the will of Heaven, loving universally and benefiting others, will obtain rewards, while

[1] *Mo-tzŭ* xiv (Mei, pp. 79 f.; Forke, pp. 242 f.; Tomkinson, p. 49).

whoso resists the will of Heaven, by being partial and harming others, will incur punishment.'¹ But the context indicates that here Mo-tzŭ is thinking of the emperor. He goes on to speak of the good emperors who received a reward and of the bad emperors who received punishment. He then continues by indicating that the reward the good received was the affection and loyalty of their people, so that they had the heritage of the empire, and were 'succeeded by descendants for ten thousand generations to continue the spread of their righteousness all over the world.'² Here the reward was the high honour of a sacred responsibility and a God-given task. There is nothing to suggest that an ignoble utilitarianism was all that was in the Sage's thought.

Part of the profit when this love was universalized would be the abolition of war. The prophets of Israel looked forward to the time when swords should be beaten into ploughshares. Our modern world wistfully yearns for the age of enduring peace. Is it something contemptible and merely utilitarian when Mo-tzŭ holds out before men the ideal of peace? He says: 'Today feudal lords know only how to love their own states and not those of others. Therefore they do not scruple to attack other states. The heads of houses know only how to love their own houses and not those of others. Therefore they do not scruple to usurp other houses. . . . When feudal lords love one another there will be no more war; when heads of houses love one another there will be no more mutual usurpation.'³

The picture of bliss which Mo-tzŭ sets before men is in notable ways comparable with that of the Old Testament passages at which we have looked. It was conceived of as resting on changed persons, as much as the pictures of the prophets were. It was not something that would come of itself, but that would come when men were worthy of it. Where Mo-tzŭ fell short was not in the loftiness of his conception of the Golden Age, or in his recognition that when all men loved their neighbours as themselves it

---

¹ *Mo-tzŭ* xxvi (Mei, p. 137; Forke, p. 317; Tomkinson, p. 86).
² *Mo-tzŭ* xxvi (Mei, p. 138; Forke, pp. 317 f.; Tomkinson, p. 86).
³ *Mo-zŭ* xv (Mei, p. 81; Forke, p. 244; Tomkinson, p. 50).

could be attained, but in his foundations for this mutual love. But to that we shall return.

Like the Confucian Sages, Mo-tzŭ put much faith in the power of example. He said 'If there were one who would establish his name for justice in the world and draw the feudal lords to him with his virtue, the submission of the whole world to him could be expected forthwith,'[1] Such optimism is too simple and too shallow. 'When a man loves others' he said, 'they love him in return; when a man profits others, they profit him in return.'[2] Or again, 'If superiors delighted in it (i.e. universal love), and promoted it by rewards and praise, and discouraged its opposite by punishments and fines, I believe people would move towards universal mutual love and the mutual sharing of benefits, as fire rises upwards and water flows downwards.'[3] The transformation of men that the Golden Age demands before it can be realized is a much more difficult task than this, and neither the Confucian Sages nor Mo-tzŭ seems to have apprehended its real nature and difficulty.

In one other important respect Mo-tzŭ may be compared with the Hebrew prophets more closely than the Confucians. He spoke much of the Will of Heaven as the foundation of it all. It was not merely because the way of love was good, or because it would be profitable when all walked in it, that he called men to it. It was because the way of love was the Will of Heaven. I have said that Confucius believed that the mandate of Heaven was upon him, but having said that he believed that it was for him to carry out that mandate. Mo-tzŭ's appeal was to the Will of Heaven, not simply as the ground of his mandate, but as the basis of the life to which he called men. If we may substitute God for Heaven, it was because God willed that men should love and live in peace and well-being that this was the right way for them. Here is something closely akin to the prophetic conception that in the will of God and in obedience to His law the true well-being of men was to be found, and that the Golden Age would be the age when that will

---

[1] *Mo-tzŭ* xix (Mei, p. 114; Forke, p. 286; Tomkinson, p. 70).
[2] *Mo-tzu* xv (Mei, p. 83; Forke, p. 248; Tomkinson, p. 50).
[3] *Mo-tzŭ* xvi (Mei, p. 97; Forke, p. 265; Tomkinson, p. 59).

should be perfectly done. He demanded righteousness, as the prophets of Israel did.[1] And he demanded it for the same reason. 'Heaven desires righteousness and abominates unrighteousness,'[2] he said, and righteousness was the standard he set before men. 'With righteousness the world lives and without it the world dies.'[3] Or again, 'If righteousness is employed in the government of the state the population will be increased, the government will be ordered, and the state will be secure. . . . Now righteousness can benefit men; hence righteousness is the finest treasure of the world.'[4] When righteousness is held before men to be their ideal, and righteousness is identified with the will of God, and when an all-embracing love for men is inculcated, and its fruits in human well-being are set forth, we have something that comes nearer to the message of the prophets of the Old Testament than anything in Confucius or Mencius, and a conception of the Golden Age that may without impropriety be called prophetic.

In Israel and in China prophets and sages were more than individualists, teaching men the good way of life, whereby they might best pass through this troubled world, and setting before men the path of their individual duty. Alike they recognized that man belongs to a society, and that his well-being is inextricably bound up with the well-being of that society. They set before men the path of duty in the society of their day, and did not live wholly in a far off Utopia. But they also perceived that the universal acceptance of the principles of righteousness and brotherhood and love which they set before men was necessary to the full attainment of the world of their vision, and also necessary to the full realization of the fruits of obedience. Neither thought simply in terms of an economic or political millennium, or conceived of the Golden Age in materialistic terms. To both it was primarily an

[1] Cf. W. Wallace, *The Chinese Recorder*, lxii, 1931, p. 559: 'His emphasis on the doctrine of righteousness is comparable to that given to it in the Old Testament.'

[2] *Mo-tzŭ* xxvi (Mei, p. 136; Forke, p. 315; Tomkinson, p. 84).

[3] *Mo-tzŭ* xxvi (Mei, p. 136). Forke (p. 315) and Tomkinson (p. 85) understand that text differently here and find the meaning to be that the righteous lives and prospers, while the unrighteous is poor and dies.

[4] *Mo-tzŭ* xlvi (Mei, p. 216; Forke, p. 542; Tomkinson, p. 125).

age of righteousness, in a world securely based on spiritual foundations. To the prophets of Israel the day of universal peace was the day when obedience to the will of God should be universal. To Mo-tzŭ it was the day when mutual love in accord with the will of Heaven should be universal. To the Confucians it was the day when righteousness and benevolence should be the foundation of the government, and when the principle of reciprocity should be accepted throughout society.

Two and half millennia after their time we still await the Golden Age, and while its glories have been promised by politicians who planned a world fit for heroes to live in, and by statesmen who fashioned a League of Nations and a United Nations Organization, to most people those glories seem still to be dim and remote. To Israel's prophets the Golden Age was God's gift to man, which could only be given when man fulfilled the conditions. To the sages of China it was man's achievement by his fulfilment of the conditions. While I would not minimize the difference between these conceptions, both alike hold the acceptance of the conditions to be essential. Only a world which sought to know and to do the will of God, as proclaimed by His servants the prophets, whether in China or in Israel, could enter into the full glories of the kingdom of God.

V

The Prophet and Worship

ITHERTO I have emphasized, and it may perhaps be felt that I have sometimes overemphasized, the points of similarity between the prophets of Israel and the three Chinese prophets of our study. I have recognized important differences as well as similarities, and in the present lecture I shall have more to say of difference than of similarity. At the outset I rejected an apologetic approach which seeks to make of the Chinese teachers a foil that sets off to greater advantage the loftiness of the Hebrew teachers. At the same time it must be remembered that it is just as much an apologetic approach that seeks to conceal the differences, though an apologetic approach with a different interest. Where there are differences, it is the way of scholarship to recognize them. Scholarship must eschew all prejudice and all unfairness in the presentation of the evidence; and this I have striven to do and will strive again now. For I approach the work of the Chinese teachers with profound esteem and sympathy, as I do also the work of the Old Testament prophets. It is not my purpose to pass a theological or religious judgement upon them, but to undertake a phenomenological study, and for this similarity and diversity are alike important.

In the previous lectures I have begun with the Israelite prophets and then turned to the Chinese teachers to see how far they displayed the qualities which the prophets of Israel showed. In the present lecture I wish to reverse the process and to begin with the Chinese teachers.

That Confucius was a great lover of ceremony and propriety needs little emphasis. When he was asked about military tactics he replied that he knew all about sacrificial vessels but was not interested in military affairs.[1] He had an expert knowledge of the rites of former days as well as of his own, and where practice diverged from that of former days, he expressed his disapproval.[2] He held in high esteem the rites[3] of the early Chou dynasty, which had behind them the rites of the Hsia and Shang dynasties, and which he regarded as 'complete and elegant'.[4] He declared that he could describe the ceremonies of the Hsia and the Shang dynasties with greater accuracy and understanding than any surviving records could match.[5] But in his day the princes were arrogating to themselves the rites proper to the emperor, and for this he had only disapproval. When he heard that the chief of the Chi family was about to sacrifice to T'ai Shan,[6] to which sacrifice could only be properly offered by the sovereign, he appealed to one of his own disciples who was in the service of the Chi family to prevent this act of impropriety.[7] When the disciple confessed his inability to do so, the Master mordantly asked if the object of the sacrifice was less discerning than Lin Fang, who had asked Confucius to say what was of the first importance in ceremonies. On another occasion Confucius condemned the head of the Chi

[1] *Analects* XV, i. i.

[2] *Analects* XI, i. This follows the interpretation of Legge, Couvreur, Pauthier, Wilhelm and Stange; cf. also Lyall. Waley, however, offers a totally different interpretation. He renders ' "Only common people wait till they are advanced in ritual and music (before taking office). A gentleman can afford to get up his ritual and music later on." Even if I accepted this saying, I should still be on the side of those who get on with their studies first.'

[3] Confucius does not here use the word for *rites*, but the word *wên*, or *culture*. In Book III of the *Analects*, however, almost every saying is concerned either with sacrifice or with ceremonial propriety, and in the light of this setting it is probable that the compilers of the *Analects* understood the meaning here to concern behaviour. Legge renders by *regulations*; Couvreur by *lois*; Wilhelm by *Ordnungen des Lebens*; Stange by *Herrschengeschlechter*.

[4] *Analects* III, xiv.

[5] *Analects* III, ix. This, again, is the rendering of Legge, Couvreur, Pauthier, Wilhelm, Lyall and Stange. But Waley, instead of rendering 'I could describe the rites . . .' has 'How can we talk about the ritual', and converts the saying into a confession of ignorance. For the sense on the usual view, cf. *Chia Yü* I, 20 b, 21 a, Section vi, § 2 (Kramers, *K'ung Tzŭ Chia Yü*, p. 221).

[6] A sacred mountain in Shantung.

[7] *Analects* III, vi.

family for having eight rows of officers to keep time in the temple services, instead of the six rows that were proper to his office.[1]

The *Doctrine of the Mean* records Confucius's eulogy of the early Chou leaders King Wu and the Duke of Chou.[2] In a long passage which commends their restoration of temples and ritual, it is said that by the regulation of the ceremonies they distinguished the ranks of men, served the dead as they would have served them alive, and served God.[3] It is added that he who understands the ceremonies of the sacrifices to Heaven and Earth, and the meaning of the several sacrifices to ancestors, would find the government of a kingdom as easy as to look into his palm.[4] This suggests that the forms of worship were regarded as useful to the government for regulating men. The disorders in the state and the impropriety in worship which Confucius deplored went hand in hand, and a restoration of the ancient ritual, performed in all cases by the right persons, would, he believed, restore the old ways.

There is a passage in the *Chia Yü* which expresses this more directly. There Confucius is said to have observed 'I have heard that of the things by which the people live the rites are greatest. But for the rites there is nothing by which to regulate the service to the spirits of Heaven and Earth. But for the rites there is nothing by which to define the positions of ruler and subject, superior and inferior, old and young. But for the rites there is nothing by which to make distinctions in the relations between male and female, father and son, elder and younger brother, the parents of the bridegroom and those of the bride, family and clan members, and the friends with whom one has infrequent or frequent contact.'[5]

The *Chia Yü* can only be used with some reserve in discussing the

---

[1] *Analects* III, i.

[2] On the Duke of Chou cf. Wilhelm, *A Short History of Chinese Civilization*, E.Tr., pp. 101 f.

[3] *The Doctrine of the Mean* xix. 4 ff.

[4] *Ibid.*, 6.

[5] *Chia Yü* I, 19 b, Section vi, § 1 (translation of Kramers, *op. cit.*, p. 220).

teaching of Confucius,[1] and in the present lectures I have made but slight use of it, and have avoided drawing on it except to reinforce what may be found elsewhere.[2] 'The *Chia Yü* can naturally not claim the same authority as the *Lun Yü*,' says Wilhelm, 'but they represent a later stage of the tradition.'[3] Where the substance of the *Chia Yü* accords with that of sayings preserved in the older books, the work may be used without unfairness to Confucius, and in the passage which I have just cited this is the case. What is implied in the passage in the *Doctrine of the Mean* is here made more explicit, and the thought is fully in accord with all we know of Confucius.

For we should note that the word *li* is rendered sometimes by *propriety* and sometimes by *rites*,[4] and that there are passages in

---

[1] Legge (*The Chinese Classics*, i, 2nd ed., p. 132) regarded it as 'a valuable fragment of antiquity', and thought 'it would be worth while to incorporate it with the *Analects*'. He accordingly drew on it freely in presenting the teaching of the Sage. Elsewhere he calls it the 'Apocryphal Analects' (*ibid.*, v, Part 2, 1872, p. 834). Others have regarded it as a forgery by Wang Su in the third century of our era. So W. Grube, *Geschichte der chinesischen Literatur*, 1902, pp. 123 f.; P. Pelliot, in *Mémoires concernant l'Asie Orientale*, ii, 1916, p. 128 n.; O. Franke, *Geschichte des chinesischen Reiches*, ii, 1936, pp. 266 f. Something between these two attitudes seems to be more satisfactory. Chavannes (*Mémoires historiques*, v, 1905, p. 439) was of the opinion that Wang Su used some ancient documents, and that the work therefore preserves some genuinely old traditions. With this view Forke is in substantial agreement (*Geschichte der alten chinesischen Philosophie*, 1927, p. 119). Wilhelm (*Confucius and Confucianism*, E.Tr., p. 74) observes that 'almost every individual section of the *Chia Yü* can be run down in the literature of the centuries between Confucius and Wang Su,' but added: 'At the same time, however, the text of the *Chia Yü* has, for the most part, a form which cannot be traced back to those texts that are now at our disposal.' After a long discussion Kramers has recently concluded that the work contained two sections, of which one consisted of older material which came into Wang Su's hands, while the other was his own composition for controversial purposes (*op. cit.*, pp. 136 f.). More cautiously, Waley says: 'Wang Su may have tampered with certain passages. But this cannot often be the case; for there are only ten paragraphs in the whole book which have not (as regards content, though not as regards phrasing) exact parallels in early literature. . . . The *Chia Yü* represents the Confucian legend as it developed during the third century B.C.' (*The Way and its Power*, 2nd ed., 1942, p. 137).

[2] Cf. Grube, *op. cit.*, p. 124: 'Als Quelle für das Leben und die Lehren des Confuzius ist das *Kia-yü* nur mit äusserster Vorsicht zu benutzen.'

[3] *Op. cit.*, p. 136.

[4] On the meanings of *li* cf. Legge, in *The Sacred Books of the East*, xxvii, 2nd impression, 1926, pp. 9 ff., and S. Couvreur, *Li Ki*, 2nd ed., i, 1913, p. ix. Also

the *Analects* where Legge uses *propriety*, but where *rites* might equally well be used, and where the same thought that religious rites are useful for regulating men may be found. In one such passage, where Legge has: 'If they (the people) be led by virtue, and uniformity sought to be given them by *the rules of propriety*, they will have the sense of shame, and moreover will become good.' Here Waley renders: 'Govern them by moral force, keep order among them by *ritual*, and they will keep their self-respect and come to you of their own accord.'[1] Similarly, in another passage, where Legge has: 'If a superior love *propriety*, the people will not dare not to be reverent,' Waley has: 'If those above love *ritual*, then among the common people none will dare to be disrespectful.'[2] Waley holds, indeed, that Confucius believed in the magical efficacy of ritual, provided it was the ancient ritual and performed by the divinely appointed ruler.[3]

On one occasion one of the chief disciples of Confucius suggested to the Master that it would be well to abolish the offering of a sheep on the first day of every month. This was because it had become a hollow ceremony, which had lost its original meaning. The Master replied: 'You love the sheep: I love the ceremony.'[4]

L. S. Hsü, *The Political Philosophy of Confucianism*, 1932, pp. 90 ff., where it is held that both *rites* and *propriety* are erroneous translations, and that the word discriminates between right and wrong, and so furnishes the foundation for legal adjudications (p. 98). E. D. Edwards (*Confucius*, 1940, p. vii) says: 'In the Confucian sense "ritual" must not be confused with religious ceremonial. Its religious significance is but one aspect of it and it must be extended to cover the whole of man's life. . . . Such phrases as . . . "order them by means of ritual" do not refer to ceremonial and rites, but imply training in the performance of actions which, because they are associated with moral and social order, tend to instil and cultivate social and moral ideals in the minds of those performing them.' L. Giles (*The Sayings of Confucius*, p. 60 n.) observes that the word *li*, as the form of the character implies, originally had sole reference to religious rites, but came to be applied to every sort of ceremonial, including the ordinary rites of politeness.

[1] *Analects* II, iii.

[2] *Analects* XIII, iv. 3. In this passage Pauthier agrees with Waley, and renders: 'Si ceux qui occupent les rangs supérieurs dans la société *aiment à observer les rites*, alors le peuple n'osera pas ne pas les respecter' (*Doctrine de Confucius*, p. 152). In the passage cited immediately above, however, Pauthier agrees more closely with Legge, and where Waley has *ritual* he has *les seules lois de la politesse sociale*.

[3] Cf. *The Analects of Confucius*, pp. 64 ff.   [4] *Analects* III, xvii.

Legge comments: 'Confucius thought that while any part of the ceremony was retained, there was a better chance of restoring the whole.'[1]

It is hard not to feel that Confucius loved religious ceremonies for their own sake, provided they conformed to the pattern laid down in the past. He said that he had no wish to look on at the great sacrifice after the pouring out of the libation,[2] and it would appear that something in the ceremony offended his sense of propriety.[3] When asked the meaning of this sacrifice, he avoided the question.[4]

What makes it apparent that he loved the ceremony for its own sake is the fact that he defended the rites of ancestor worship, while declining to commit himself as to the survival of the ancestors. We are told that he sacrificed to the dead as if they were present, and that he considered his absence from the ceremony as if he did not sacrifice.[5] Yet when he was asked about serving the spirits, he replied 'While you are not able to serve men, how can you serve their spirits?' and when his questioner continued to ask about death, he answered 'While you do not know life, how can you know about death?'[6] An incident recorded in the *Chia Yü* is wholly consistent with this. There we read that Tzŭ Kung asked him if the dead have knowledge, and he replied 'If I should say that the dead have knowledge, I am fearful that filial sons would immolate living persons to accompany the dead. If I should say that the dead have no knowledge, I am fearful that unfilial sons would throw away their parents' bodies without burying them. Ssŭ, your wish to know whether or not the dead have knowledge is not an urgent problem of the present; later on you will know it as a matter of course.'[7] Legge sternly condemns Confucius for this want of candour, and inclines to think that he doubted more than he believed.[8]

---

[1] *The Chinese Classics*, i, 2nd ed., p. 161.   [2] *Analects* III, x.
[3] Cf. Waley's note (*The Analects of Confucius*, p. 96 n.).   [4] *Analects* III, xi.
[5] *Analects* III, xii.   [6] *Analects* XI, xi.
[7] *Chia Yü* I, 10 b, Section viii, § 17 (translation of Kramers, *K'ung Tzŭ Chia Yü*, p. 238).
[8] Cf. *The Chinese Classics*, i, 2nd ed., pp. 99 f.

Certainly some of his followers in a later age doubted, though they continued to observe the sacrifices. This appears in one of Mo-tzŭ's criticisms. In the course of his discussion with a Confucianist Kung-Mêng-tzŭ, the latter, we are told, said that ghosts and spirits are non-existent, yet advocated that the superior man should learn sacrifice and worship. To Mo-tzŭ this was both insincere and futile. He said 'To hold that there are no spirits and yet learn sacrificial rites is comparable to learning the ceremonials of hospitality while refusing to entertain a guest or to making fishing nets while denying the existence of fish.'[1]

There is a cryptic passage which is held to indicate that Confucius had little use for prayer. We are told that when he was ill, the disciple Tzŭ Lu asked leave to pray for him; but Confucius remarked 'My praying has been for a long time.'[2] Legge observes that this remark seems to indicate Confucius's satisfaction with himself, and this rests on the orthodox commentary of Chu Hsi, which Legge cites as 'Prayer is the expression of repentance and promise of amendment, to supplicate the help of the spirits. If there be not these things, then there is no need for praying. In the case of the sage, he had committed no errors, and admitted of no amendment. In all his conduct he had been in harmony with the spiritual intelligences, and therefore he said—my praying has been for a long time.'[3] This would appear to interpret the cryptic remark to mean 'My praying was all over long ago.' It is by no means certain, however, that this is the meaning, and the words might well be understood to mean that he had been praying already for a long time.[4]

[1] *Mo-tzu* xlviii (Mei, p. 236; Forke, p. 569; Tomkinson, p. 139).
[2] *Analects* VII, xxxiv.   [3] *The Chinese Classics*, i, 2nd ed., p. 206.
[4] Cf. the rendering of Pauthier: 'La prière de Khieou (la sienne) est permanente'; Lyall: 'Long-lasting has been my prayer'; Couvreur: 'Il y a longtemps que je prie.' Couvreur adds a note which says: 'Ma prière est vraiment continuelle. Comment aurais-je attendu jusqu' aujourd'hui (pour prier)?' Waley is in closer agreement with Legge, and comments: 'What justifies me in the eyes of Heaven is the life I have led. There is no need for any rite now.' Cf. L. Giles (*The Sayings of Confucius*, p. 87), who renders 'My prayers began long ago' and comments 'His whole life had been one long prayer, and he refuses any mediation between himself and God.'

We are told that whenever he ate, though his food might be simple and coarse, he always offered a little in sacrifice with a grave respectful air.[1] But this could be as devoid of real meaning as the grace which is often said at meat in our day. A story which is recorded in the *Chia Yü* is worth repeating. It tells how a fisherman once offered Confucius a fish, which the Sage refused. When the fisherman observed that the day was hot and it was far to the nearest market, so that he had thought it would be better to offer it to him than to throw it away, Confucius accepted the gift and at once made preparations to perform a sacrifice with it. When one of the disciples questioned the propriety of this, Confucius replied that the fisherman had shown the quality of goodness, and asked 'How could there be one who, on receiving a food-present from a good man, would not perform a sacrifice with it?'[2] It will be observed that here the sacrifice was less the means of offering worship to God than a tribute to the spirit of the fisherman.

Before we dismiss Confucius, however, as an insincere formalist, we may note a few utterances with a more prophetic flavour. When he interpreted a line of an ancient poem[3] to mean 'The business of laying on the colours follows the preparation of the plain ground', his disciple understood this to mean 'that ceremonies are a subsequent thing', and in characteristic fashion Confucius expressed his approval of this.[4] Here, once more, we have a cryptic passage, but it would appear to mean that ceremonies are secondary, and Waley understands this to mean that they can only be built upon goodness.[5] This is in harmony with another saying: 'If a man be without the virtues proper to humanity, what has he to do with the rites of propriety?'[6] To these may be

---

[1] *Analects* X, viii. 10. Waley here understands the text quite differently, and renders: 'Any article of food, whether coarse rice, vegetables, broth or melon, that has been used as an offering must be handled with due solemnity.'

[2] *Chia Yü* II, 2 b, 3 a, Section viii, § 3 (translation of Kramers, *op. cit.*, p. 232).

[3] Supposed to be a poem which Confucius did not include in the *Shih Ching*, though part of the passage cited is found there, but without the conclusion.

[4] *Analects* III, viii.   [5] Cf. *The Analects of Confucius*, p. 96 n.

[6] *Analects* III, iii. Waley here renders: 'A man who is not Good, what can he have to do with ritual?'

added a passage from the *Li Chi*, which Legge renders: 'With a superior man the use of ceremonies is to give proper and elegant expression to the feelings.'[1] While this is meagre evidence, it would seem to point to the conclusion that Confucius valued not the ceremony alone, but the life and character of the man who offered it, and the spirit with which he came to it. Wilhelm says: 'All forms without the basic truth of inner attitude are empty and despicable. For Confucius, indeed, this inner attitude transcends in importance the perfection of external form.'[2] In harmony with this is the noble saying which I have already quoted: 'He who offends against Heaven has none to whom he can pray.'[3] While his spirit is offensive to Heaven no act of worship can have any meaning. Already in the *Shu Ching* we find this thought expressed. In one passage we read: 'The spirits do not always accept the sacrifices which are offered to them. They accept only the sacrifices of the sincere.'[4] In another we find: 'If the observances are not equal to the articles, it must be said there is no offering. When there is no service of the will in the offerings of the princes, all the people will then say, "We need not be troubled about our offerings".'[5] Hollow sacrifices can deceive neither spirits nor men.

Of Mencius it is unnecessary to treat at length. Forke says that Mencius had more heart than Confucius, and finds a closer sympathy between him and the western spirit.[6] He was less interested in religion, however, and for the forms of religion he seems to have cared but little. Legge says: 'Never once, where he is treating of the nature of man, does he make mention of any exercise of the mind as due directly to God.'[7] He adds: 'The services of religion come in China under the principle of propriety, and are only a cold formalism; but even here, other things come with

---

[1] *Li Chi* v, Sect. 2, 7 (translation of Legge in *The Sacred Books of the East*, xxvii, p. 331). Couvreur renders: 'Les démonstrations extérieures sont pour le sage comme (la fleur et) la parure des sentiments de son cœur' (in *Li Ki*, i, 2nd ed., p. 445).
[2] *Confucius and Confucianism*, pp. 144 ff.　　　　　[3] *Analects* III, xiii. 2.
[4] *Shu Ching* IV Book 5, Part 3, i. 1 (Legge's rendering).
[5] *Shu Ching* V Book 13, iii. 12 (Legge's rendering).
[6] Cf. *Geschichte der alten chinesischen Philosophie*, p. 194.
[7] *The Chinese Classics*, ii, 2nd ed., p. 72.

Mencius before them.'[1] In support of this he cites a passage in which filial piety and brotherly service are commended, after which it is declared that wisdom lies in observing these two things and propriety in adorning them.[2] Such evidence as we have, therefore, suggests that Mencius had little use for worship as a vital religious experience.

We should, however, note that he insists on the necessity for sincerity in sacrifice, and directs attention to the spirit of the one who offers sacrifice as essential to the valid performance of the rite. He says: 'Though a man may be wicked, yet if he adjust his thoughts, fast, and bathe, he may sacrifice to God.'[3]

That brilliant writer, Wang Ch'ung, whom Wieger calls the greatest genius of all Chinese writers[4] and Wilhelm 'that sceptical eccentric',[5] dismissed all sacrifice as useless and futile,[6] and declared that everything depended on man and his virtue and not on sacrifice.[7] This is an attitude to religious forms which some, as we shall see, have attributed to the prophets of Israel. There was, however, a world of difference between his thought and theirs, since his rested on a denial of the existence of God or spirits,[8] and he lies farther from the prophets of the Old Testament than Confucius or Mencius.

---

[1] *Ibid.*   [2] *Mencius* IV Part 1, xxvii.

[3] *Mencius* IV Part 2, xxv. 2.

[4] *Histoire des Croyances religieuses*, p. 318. On Wang Ch'ung cf. A. Forke, *Lun-Hêng*, i, 1907, Introduction, and *Geschichte der mittelalterlichen chinesischen Philosophie*, 1934, pp. 110 ff. In the latter work, p. 114, Forke cites the words of Mayers (published in 1874, and not accessible to the present writer): 'Wang Ch'ung, a philosopher, perhaps the most original and judicious among all the metaphysicians China has produced . . . who . . . handles mental and physical problems in a style and with a boldness unparalleled in Chinese literature.' Cf. also Fung Yu-lan, *A History of Chinese Philosophy*, E.Tr. by D. Bodde, ii, 1953, pp. 150 ff. On p. 151 Fung says: 'Because his ideas were primarily destructive rather than constructive, their intrinsic value is less than some recent scholars have supposed.'

[5] *A Short History of Chinese Civilization*, E.Tr. by Joan Joshua, 1929, p. 178.

[6] Cf. Forke, *Lun-Hêng*, i, pp. 509 ff.   [7] Cf. Forke, *ibid.*, p. 535.

[8] Cf. Forke, *ibid.*, p. 18, where Wang Ch'ung's views are summarized as being that Heaven is without a mind, and is unaffected by men and indifferent to their prayers. Cf. also p. 287: 'We try to get a conception of Heaven by ascribing human qualities to it. The source of this knowledge of Heaven is man.'

To Mo-tzŭ the spirits of the dead were real, and he had no doubt whatever that they continued to exist. Indeed, he insists on this in one of the surviving Synoptic Chapters, and adduces a number of passages from ancient annals to prove their effective activity after death.[1] When, therefore, he insists that men should prepare clean cakes and wine and do sacrifice with reverence,[2] he is not thinking of a hollow ceremony, which is good discipline for the living, but of genuine worship, and he records the punishment meted out to one who failed to bring clean cakes and wine to these sacrifices.[3] 'For me to offer sacrifice', he said, 'is not to throw it into the ditch or the gully. It is to bless the spirits above and gather a party and enjoy ourselves and befriend the neighbours below. And if spirits exist, I supply my father and mother and brother with food. Is not this a great blessing in the world?'[4]

Nevertheless Mo-tzŭ said little on the forms of worship. He appears to have accepted existing forms, as Confucius and Mencius did, save that Confucius wished to restore them to their ancient observance. But whereas Mencius was largely indifferent to the forms of worship, giving them not more than passing recognition, and Confucius stressed them but emptied them of any true worship of spiritual beings, Mo-tzŭ desired them to be genuinely forms of worship. All were more concerned with the lives of men than they were with worship. To Confucius it was but a tool to be used for the reform of men and of manners. Mencius was content with the appeal to reason and conscience to effect that reform. Mo-tzŭ reinforced this by the appeal to God more than either of the others, but it was to the idea and will of God much more than the worship of God that he turned.

Here, once more, we may find some immediate points of contact and similarity with the Hebrew prophets. They said little in commendation of the forms of worship, and were not primarily

[1] Mo-tzŭ xxxi (Mei, pp. 160 ff.; Forke, pp. 343 ff.; Tomkinson, pp. 100 ff.).
[2] Mo-tzŭ xxxi (Mei, p. 173; Forke, p. 363; Tomkinson, p. 109).
[3] Mo-tzŭ xxxi (Mei, p. 164; Forke, p. 349; Tomkinson, p. 102 f.).
[4] Mo-tzŭ xxxi (Mei, p. 174; Forke, p. 364; Tomkinson, pp. 110).

concerned for the ritual observances of the shrines. Of the reality of God they were in no doubt, and of this we shall think in our last lecture. They would have repudiated Confucius's interest in the ceremonies for their own sake, though they would have shared his view that ceremonies were secondary to the life of those who partook of them. They would have shared Mo-tzŭ's view that in so far as the forms of religion were observed they should be the vehicle of genuine worship, and not a hollow pretence. They would not have dispensed with prayer, but they would have approved of the saying that the man who offends against God has none to whom he can pray, so long as he clings to his offence. Indeed, we may bring into direct connection with this the word of Isaiah: 'When ye spread forth your hands, I will hide mine eyes from you: yea, when ye make many prayers, I will not hear: your hands are full of blood.'[1]

The prophets of Israel, however, made much more radical attacks on the forms of worship of their contemporaries than any of these Chinese teachers. The things that Confucius condemned were the usurpations of rites by the princes, or modifications of the ceremonies as compared with the ceremonies of the past. It was the incorrectness of the ritual that was the offensive thing to him. As a ceremony it was imperfect. The Hebrew prophets, however, were not concerned with the ritual as a mere ceremony, and so far as one can judge the ceremonies they condemned as offensive to God were offered with every technical propriety.

In the time of Amos splendid sacrifices were being offered, with every accompaniment of song. Yet the prophet could say in the name of God 'I hate, I despise your feasts, and I will take no delight in your solemn assemblies. Yea, though ye offer me your burnt offerings and meal offerings, I will not accept them: neither will I regard the peace offerings of your fat beasts. Take thou away from me the noise of thy songs; for I will not hear the melody of thy viols.'[2] Similarly Isaiah could say 'To what purpose is the multitude of your sacrifices unto me? saith the Lord; I am full of the burnt offerings of rams, and the fat of fed beasts

[1] Isa. i. 15.   [2] Amos v. 21 ff.

and I delight not in the blood of bullocks, or of lambs or of he-goats.'[1] In the book of Micah we have an oracle which is held by many to be from another nameless prophet, though for our purpose it does not matter whether it was uttered by Micah or another.[2] It asks 'Wherewith shall I come before the Lord, and bow myself before the high God? Shall I come before him with burnt offerings, with calves of a year old? Will the Lord be pleased with thousands of rams, or with ten thousands of rivers of oil?'[3] It is quite clear that the answer to these rhetorical questions is 'Certainly not.' Or yet again, Jeremiah says 'To what purpose cometh there to me frankincense from Sheba, and the sweet cane from a far country? Your burnt offerings are not acceptable, nor your sacrifices pleasing unto me.'[4]

Here is an array of passages which cannot be matched from the Chinese sources, and which can easily give the impression that the prophets were totally opposed to the whole institution of sacrifice, and regarded it as an unmitigated evil. There have not been wanting scholars who have maintained that this was the position they adopted. A single example may here suffice. Emil Kautzsch, in a well-known article on the religion of Israel, said 'No one has any right to depreciate the merit which belongs to the above-named prophets, of having discovered the ideal of true service of God in the worship of Him in spirit and in truth, without any outward ceremonies and performances.'[5] It is hard to think of a religion without any shrines or places of worship, and without any means of expressing itself in worship; but we must not on that ground rule out this view of the prophets. If this is correct, the prophets of Israel stand alongside Mencius most closely,

[1] Isa. i. 11 ff.

[2] In *The Growth of the Old Testament*, 1950, p. 116, I said that I am not inclined to pronounce for or against Micah's authorship. Cf. A. George, *Michée, Sophonie, Nahum*, 1952, p. 12: 'On ne refuse plus de lui (i.e. to Micah) attribuer en outre des fragments importants en v. 8–vii. 7.'

[3] Mic. vi. 6 f.   [4] Jer. vi. 20.

[5] Hastings's *D.B.*, Extra Volume, 1904, p. 686 b. Cf. also J. P. Hyatt, *Prophetic Religion*, 1947, p. 127: 'The opposition of the prophets to the whole sacrificial and ritualistic system and practices of their day seems to have been absolute, and they thought it should be abolished as an offense against the God of Israel.'

concerned for wise government, concerned for the oppressed people, eager to see moral principles given expression in the life of his day, but fundamentally indifferent to worship. The only notable difference from Mencius would then be that while he ignored the question of worship, they actively opposed it. To the passages I have cited we may now add a well-known passage in Hosea, which says 'I desire mercy, and not sacrifice; and the knowledge of God more than burnt offerings.'[1] It would be possible grammatically to translate the second part of this 'And the knowledge of God *without* burnt offerings', and there are not wanting those who would so translate it.[2]

I have more than once expressed my disagreement with this view of the prophets,[3] but it is necessary briefly to examine it here. It is a view which has found the support of many distinguished scholars, and it cannot be brushed lightly aside. Micah predicted the destruction of the Temple,[4] and a century later Jeremiah did the same thing.[5] Both of these could conceive of religion continuing without any shrine in which it could function, and it must be remembered that the Jews who were exiled in Babylon had no temple or sacrificial cultus, and there was no synagogue yet at the time of the exile.[6] It was that rich quality of *ḥesedh*, which

[1] Hos. vi. 6.

[2] So S. Herner, *Sühne und Vergebung in Israel*, 1942, p. 36; E. C. B. Maclaurin, *The Origin of the Hebrew Sacrificial System*, 1948, p. 29.

[3] Cf. *B.J.R.L.*, xxix, 1945–6, pp. 326 ff., xxxiii, 1950–1, pp. 74 ff., and *The Unity of the Bible*, 1953, pp. 30 ff.

[4] Mic. iii. 12.

[5] Jer. vii. 14, xxvi. 6.

[6] L. E. Browne, in *J.T.S.*, xvii, 1916, pp. 400 f., and *Early Judaism*, 1920, p. 53, argued that Ezra viii. 17 may contain a reference to a Jewish Temple in Babylonia, where Ezra's brother was a priest. As for the synagogue, it is commonly believed that it came into existence in Babylonia amongst the exiles, though there is no definite evidence for this. Cf. W. Bacher, *Jewish Encyclopedia*, xi, 1905, p. 619 b.; G. F. Moore, *Judaism*, i, 1927, p. 283; A. Menes, *Z.A.W.*, N.F. ix, 1932, pp. 268 ff. S. Zeitlin, in *P.A.A.J.R.*, ii, 1931, pp. 69 ff., maintains that the synagogue did not come into being until after the exile, and that it was a secular meeting place at first. If Torrey's reading on an ostracon is correct (*B.A.S.O.R.*, No. 84, Dec. 1941, pp. 4 f.), the earliest known evidence for the existence of a synagogue comes from Elath. This ostracon is dated by Albright at the end of the sixth century B.C. (*ibid.*, No. 82, April 1941, pp. 11 ff.).

is something more than our word mercy connotes,[1] which Hosea called for. Similarly in that passage in the book of Micah, what is demanded instead of burnt offerings and rivers of oil is expressed in the words 'He hath shewed thee, O man, what is good; and what doth the Lord require of thee, but to do justly, to love *hesedh*, and to walk humbly with thy God.'[2] Amos follows up his denunciation of the sacrifices by saying 'But let judgement roll down as waters, and righteousness as a mighty—or, better, as a neverfailing—stream.'[3] Isaiah closes his denunciation of the sacrifices and ceremonies of his day by crying 'Wash you, make you clean; put away the evil of your doings from before mine eyes; cease to do evil: learn to do well; seek judgement, relieve the oppressed, judge the fatherless, plead for the widow.'[4]

In all these passages, then, we seem to have a passionate call for righteousness and a spirit of true human brotherhood in life, coupled with a repudiation of all the forms of worship. There is greater moral passion in the call for human brotherhood than we find in Confucius and Mencius, and a greater heat against the ritual forms of worship than we find in any of the Chinese teachers.

We must, however, notice that Isaiah's denunciation includes not merely sacrifices and festivals, but also prayer. He says 'When ye spread forth your hands, I will hide mine eyes from you; yea, when ye make many prayers, I will not hear.'[5] Prayer stands under the same condemnation as the sacrificial cultus, so that if the one is absolute, the other is equally absolute. Jeremiah can scarcely be credited with such an attitude to prayer, for he well knew the experience of prayer. He could have prayed without the Temple, of course, and there is no reason to suppose that his recorded prayers were offered in the Temple. We might therefore suppose that when Isaiah denounced prayer along with the sacrifices, all he meant was that the prayers of the Temple were an abomination

---

[1] Cf. above, p. 56.

[2] Mic. vi. 8. A. George, *Michée, Sophonie, Nahum*, p. 39, observes: 'Cette triple exigence, d'ordre tout spirituel, correspond précisément aux revendications fondamentales des trois grand prophètes antérieurs à Michée.'

[3] Amos v. 24.   [4] Isa. i. 16 f.   [5] Isa. i. 15.

to God, and that he could have contemplated the continuance of private prayer. Against such a view there are several important considerations. In the first place Isaiah was not opposed to the Temple. His own inaugural vision was in the Temple,[1] and throughout his life he proclaimed that the Temple should be spared, and for its sake Jerusalem.[2] It cannot be supposed that he thought the Temple should continue to exist as the House of God but should be completely deserted by men; and if men frequented it, it could only be for worship. In the second place, he finished up his denunciation by saying 'Your hands are full of blood.'[3] If he had meant that God hated sacrifices, sacred festivals and prayer under all circumstances, then the blood-stained hands had nothing to do with it, and should not have been introduced to cloud the issue. If these words were essential to his thought, then it would seem that he meant that the worship was unacceptable because the lives of the worshippers were hateful to God, and not because the worship was offered in the Temple. In the third place, although Jeremiah could contemplate the destruction of the Temple, he did not think the Temple was necessarily evil. For he announced that if men repented and amended their ways, the Temple might be spared.[4] Had it been wholly evil and all its worship hateful in the

[1] Isa. vi. 1.

[2] Cf. Isa. iv. 5 f., xxxi. 5, xxxiii. 20 ff. Cf. also Isa. i. 8, which is commonly held to date from the time of Sennacherib's campaign of 701 B.C., since this provides the only known occasion which is appropriate to the passage. Other dates during Isaiah's ministry, however, have found some advocates.   [3] Isa. i. 15.

[4] Jer. vii. 3. J. Skinner (*Prophecy and Religion*, 1922, pp. 170 f.) holds that vii. 3–7 are a supplementary composition by a Deuteronomic commentator. On literary grounds this is hard to establish in view of the universally recognized links of style that bind Jeremiah and Deuteronomy. The real ground of Skinner's objection is his firm conviction that Jeremiah was irrevocably opposed to the Temple cultus under any circumstances, and anything that conflicts with this must be excised from the book. So he argues that if every element that conflicts with such a view is eliminated from this chapter, then we have only 'an *absolute* prediction of the devastation of the *sanctuary* and the rejection of the nation'. He then proceeds to eliminate the condition in the parallel Jer. xxvi. 2 ff., on the ground that it is excluded by the text in chapter vii as it leaves Skinner's hands. This is to impose a theory on the text, rather than to find support for it from the text. Other scholars have found no difficulty in accepting the text as Jeremianic. So Peake, *Jeremiah*, i, pp. 145 ff.

eyes of God, then surely the prophet should have wished to see it destroyed anyhow, and it could not be a mark of divine mercy to leave it.

It is then to be observed that in all the prophetic denunciations of sacrifice there is reference to iniquity of life. The words should not be taken by themselves, but read in connection with the rest of the prophetic message. Amos notes the lack of righteousness,[1] and elsewhere in his short book we have ample evidence of the unrighteousness and exploitation that prevailed.[2] Hosea brings into association with one another his demand for ḥesedh and his denunciation of sacrifice.[3] Jeremiah introduces the declaration that the sacrifices of his day are not acceptable to God by complaining that men had not hearkened to the word of God and had rejected His law.[4] It would therefore seem that the reason for the condemnation of the ritual acts was the manner of life of the people who resorted to the Temple for their performance, and we ought not to conclude that it was the ritual acts which were themselves, and under all circumstances, condemned.

There is one passage in Jeremiah which I have not yet cited, which is often held to be the most absolute in its condemnation of sacrifice. It reads 'I spake not unto your fathers, nor commanded them in the day that I brought them out of the land of Egypt, concerning burnt offerings or sacrifices; but this thing I commanded them, saying, Hearken unto my voice, and I will be your God, and ye shall be my people; and walk ye in all the way that I command you, that it may be well with you.'[5] But this passage is only an echo of a passage in Exodus: 'If ye will obey my voice indeed, and keep my covenant, then ye shall be a peculiar treasure unto me from among all peoples.'[6] This was the first demand of God, more fundamental than any demand for sacrifice, even in the early document of the Pentateuch in which this passage

---

[1] Amos v. 24.   [2] Cf. Amos ii. 6 ff., iii. 9 f., v. 11 f., viii. 4 ff.
[3] Hos. vi. 6.   [4] Jer. vi. 19.   [5] Jer. vii. 22 f.
[6] According to S. R. Driver (*Introduction to the Literature of the Old Testament*, 9th ed., 1913, p. 31) and Oesterley and Robinson (*Introduction to the Books of the Old Testament*, 1934, p. 37), this verse comes from the oldest of the main documents of the Pentateuch. Others, however, assign it to the hand of a later redactor.

stands.[1] That document goes on to prescribe sacrifices, but it does not give them the place of first importance. It is probable that we should similarly find in the passage in Jeremiah the declaration that God's demand for obedience is primary, and more important than any demand for the forms of worship. The apparently absolute terms which are employed do not preclude a comparative meaning. For this is characteristic of Hebrew idiom. In the New Testament Jesus declares that no man can be His disciple unless he hates his father and mother.[2] The apparently absolute terms are readily perceived to mean that He demands a love greater than that felt for the nearest kin.[3] Many other examples of this idiom could be cited,[4] and in the light of it we may with probability understand these prophetic passages to mean that sacrifice has no meaning merely as an act in itself unrelated to the spirit of the one who offers it.

This view has found an increasing number of supporters in recent years. It may suffice here to cite two. Wheeler Robinson observed: 'For the prophets everything depended on the spirit in which an act was performed. . . . Similarly we may say that they condemned the *opus operatum* of sacrifice, so long as it was not lifted up into the spirit of true devotion to Yahweh, and the true obedience to His moral requirements';[5] while W. A. Irwin, in speaking of Amos, says: 'It was not ritual as such to which he objected, but rather the practice of ritual by people who believed that thereby they set in motion magical forces and insured for

[1] Exod. xix. 5.

[2] Luke xiv. 26.

[3] This is what we find in the parallel passage in Matt. x. 37.

[4] Cf. C. J. Cadoux, *E.T.*, lii, 1940–1, pp. 378 f.; C. Lattey, *J.T.S.*, xlii, 1941, pp. 158 ff. Cf. Mark ix. 37: 'Whosoever receiveth me receiveth not me but him that sent me'; John vii. 16: 'My teaching is not mine, but his that sent me'; John vi. 27: 'Work not for the meat which perisheth, but for the meat which abideth unto eternal life'; Gen. xlv. 8: 'It was not you that sent me hither, but God.' In all these cases the meaning of the negative is 'not so much', and the sentence is fundamentally comparative. It is therefore in full accord with this idiomatic construction to take the text in Jeremiah to mean 'I did not command sacrifice so much as obedience', and to find the essential meaning to be in agreement with that of I Sam. xv. 22.

[5] *J.T.S.*, xliii, 1942, p. 137.

themselves well-being and happiness.'[1] If this is correct, it means
that the prophets were dominantly interested in summoning men
to obedience to the will of God in all their life, and this obedience
consisted in the reflection of the character of God in so far as it may
be reflected under the conditions of human life, and that they had
no use whatever for worship as an act in itself, unrelated to life.
To them worship was fundamentally the presenting of oneself
before God, rather than merely presenting one's sacrifice before
Him. It is quite inconceivable that any of them would have boasted
an expert knowledge of sacrificial vessels, as Confucius did,[2] or
would have wished to preserve a sacrificial rite which had become a hollow form. It was against hollow forms that they continually protested, for worship was to be sought in the spirit
much more than in the act.

Nor is there the slightest evidence that these great pre-exilic
prophets were interested in the demand for worthy sacrifices,
comparable with Mo-tzŭ's concern about clean cakes and wine.[3]
But here in fairness it should be said that amongst the post-exilic
prophets we find a spirit comparable with Mo-tzŭ's. Malachi
complained that men were bringing polluted bread and indifferent
sacrifices to the Temple, instead of bringing animals without
blemish.[4] It was no honour to God to bring Him their second
best, instead of their best. Here we should remember that every
prophet speaks to his own age. In the eighth century it was not
the poverty of the sacrifices that was the problem, but the spirit
with which men brought to God the most splendid sacrifices.
Sacrifices which in themselves were most worthy were made
valueless by the spirit in which they were brought. In the time of
Malachi the devotion men professed with their lips was belied
by the indifference of the offerings they brought. In the time of
Mo-tzŭ it would appear that the Sage found something of the
same spirit.

---

[1] In J. M. Powis Smith, *The Prophets and their Times*, 2nd ed., revised by W. A.
Irwin, 1941, p. 62.   [2] *Analects* XV, i. 1.
[3] *Mo-tzŭ* xxxi (Mei, pp. 164, 173; Forke, pp. 349, 263; Tomkinson, pp. 102 f.
109).   [4] Mal. i. 7 ff.

It is commonly agreed that the post-exilic prophets were men of lesser stature than the great pre-exilic prophets. If Mo-tzŭ can be set with the post-exilic prophets here, we may go on to ask whether he and the other Chinese teachers should not be placed far below the eighth- and seventh-century prophets of Israel so far as their conception of worship is concerned. And the answer is an unhesitating Yes. In none of the Chinese teachers do we find the depth of meaning given to worship which we find in the Israelite prophets. For the question of their attitude to sacrifice and to the cultus of the Temple is but one part of the question of their attitude to worship. To them worship was something much wider than an act in the Temple; it belonged to all life. I have said that Confucius recognized that goodness was more fundamental than ritual, and both Mencius and Mo-tzŭ would have agreed with this. But to the Israelite prophets the obedience to the will of God in the common ways of life to which they called men was more than obedience to a word. It was itself worship. To them God was intensely personal, and the essence of worship consisted in a personal relationship to Him, a relationship which might be renewed in the shrine, but which must be continued outside the shrine.

They represented God as loving Israel in a richly personal way. 'You only have I known of all the families of the earth' said Amos.[1] And Hosea pictures God as a father teaching his little son to walk.[2] Similarly Isaiah thinks of Israel as children whom God has reared and brought up.[3] All were sure that Israel had ill requited that love and had been rebellious children, running away from their Father, plunging into iniquity. Yet God in His love pursued them with His mercy, sending His prophets to recall them to Himself, 'rising up early and sending them', as Jeremiah expresses it in finely anthropomorphic language.[4]

To the prophets, therefore, worship consisted in a personal relationship to this God. Isaiah complained that men drew near to God with their mouths and honoured Him with their lips, but

[1] Amos iii. 2.   [2] Hos. xi. 3.   [3] Isa. i. 2.
[4] Jer. vii. 13, 25; xi. 7; xxv. 4; xxvi. 5; xxix. 19; xxxii. 33; xxxv. 14 f.; xliv. 4.

their hearts were far from Him.[1] It was not that they were worshipping Him with the wrong ritual, but that the personal relationship was wrong. At his own call Isaiah saw the Lord in the Temple,[2] and in an experience whose religious profundity is unmatched in the experience of any Chinese teacher brought a depth of worship that reveals something of the real meaning of worship. So far as our record goes, the experience was not associated with any ritual act in which Isaiah played a part. The worship which he brought to God consisted in the yielding of his whole personality to the service of God. At the vision of God he cried 'Woe is me! for I am undone; for I am a man of unclean lips, and I dwell in the midst of a people of unclean lips: for mine eyes have seen the King, the Lord of hosts.'[3] The vision brought home to him his need of spiritual renewal and his inability to effect it himself, and filled him with the sense that in that holy presence sin could not live, and that therefore he must perish with his sin. Here is nothing of the proud and hard spirit of those whose sacrifices the prophets condemned—men who provided the gifts they brought with what they unrighteously extorted from others, and who came before God with no sense of their need, because they had no eyes to behold the God before whom they stood. To Isaiah, whose heart was filled with exaltation at the vision granted him and with trembling at the sense of his unworthiness, there was mediated cleansing and the renewal of his being. 'Thine iniquity is taken away, and thy sin purged.'[4] And then Isaiah yielded the cleansed and renewed self in consecration to the God he had seen.[5] Here we see the true meaning of worship in the shrine. The ritual act is secondary to this traffic of the soul with God, bringing inspiration and issuing in consecration. And then the sequel to the worship lies in the life to which it leads, the life which is not confined to the shrine.

Moreover, the life itself may be continued worship, since the relationship with the personal God is not confined to the shrine, though it may find its most exalted moments there. In the passage

[1] Isa. xxix. 13.   [2] Isa. vi. 1.   [3] Isa. vi. 5.
[4] Isa. vi. 7.   [5] Isa. vi. 8.

in the book of Micah which I have already quoted, the prophet
defines the supreme demand of God as for the doing of justice,
the loving of *hesedh*, and the humble walk with God.[1] The
Chinese Sages might have asked for the first two of these, but
they would not have asked for the third. The Israelite prophet
perceived that it could only be by the fellowship of God that
resource could be found for the obedience to God. Running
through much of the Old Testament we find this emphasis on the
fellowship of God as the privilege of men. 'The Lord was with
Joseph.'[2] 'Certainly I will be with thee.'[3] 'I am with thee to deliver thee.'[4] The eye must be open to see God if the experience is
to be had, and the heart must be full of the spirit of worship and
ready to let worship lead to obedience.

It is by this larger sense of the meaning of worship that the
prophets are distinguished. Especially do we find this inner communion with God exemplified in the experience of Jeremiah, who
more than any other of the prophets understood the significance
of prayer. We have little record of the prayers of the other prophets, but prayer figures frequently in the story of Jeremiah, and
especially in the series of passages which are sometimes referred
to as the Confessions of Jeremiah.[5] Characterizing these passages,
Skinner says: 'To Jeremiah prayer is more than petition. It is
intimate converse with God, in which his whole inner life is laid
bare.'[6] The same writer observes that his first prayers were
prayers of intercession for the nation against which he was
called to prophesy.[7] From this he rose to the stage where, again
in Skinner's words, 'prayer is the effort of the soul to bring every
thought and feeling into harmony with the will of God, and to
find its true good in being right with Him'.[8] It is little wonder
that this prophet looked for the day when God's law should be
written on the hearts of men, and when all should know Him in
the intimacy of fellowship.[9]

---

[1] Mic. vi. 8.   [2] Gen. xxxix. 21.   [3] Exod. iii. 12.
[4] Jer. i. 8, 19; xv. 20.   [5] Cf. J. Skinner, *Prophecy and Religion*, pp. 201 ff.
[6] *Ibid.*, p. 213.   [7] *Ibid.*, p. 227.   [8] *Ibid.*, p. 228.
[9] Jer. xxxi. 31 ff.

Deutero-Isaiah, speaking in the period of the exile in Babylonia, where no Temple was accessible for the worship of the God
of Israel, yet understood this deeper meaning of worship. 'They
that wait upon the Lord shall renew their strength; they shall
mount up with wings as eagles; they shall run, and not be weary;
they shall walk, and not faint.'[1] 'When thou passest through the
waters I will be with thee; and through the rivers, they shall not
overflow thee; when thou walkest through the fire, thou shalt
not be burned; neither shall the flame kindle upon thee.'[2] He knew
how to hymn the praises of God. 'Sing unto the Lord a new song,
and his praise from the end of the earth.'[3] A similar song stands
in the early part of the book of Isaiah, though it is commonly
believed not to be Isaiah's.[4] For our purpose this is immaterial,
since it equally bears testimony to the prophetic recognition of
joyous thanksgiving to God as a form of worship. 'Sing unto the
Lord; for he hath done excellent things: let this be known in all
the earth. Cry aloud and shout, thou inhabitant of Zion: for great
is the Holy One of Israel in the midst of thee.'[5] We look in vain
for anything comparable with this in the records of Confucius,
Mencius or Mo-tzŭ. Nor can those records provide us with any
penetrating sense of the meaning of worship that can be set beside
the familiar passage: 'Seek ye the Lord while he may be found,
call ye upon him while he is near: let the wicked forsake his way,
and the unrighteous man his thoughts: and let him return unto
the Lord, and he will have mercy upon him; and to our God, for
he will abundantly pardon. For my thoughts are not your
thoughts, neither are your ways my ways, saith the Lord. For as

[1] Isa. xl. 21.

[2] Isa. xliii. 2.

[3] Isa. xlii. 10. J. Morgenstern (in *To Do and to Teach*, Pyatt Memorial Volume,
1953, pp. 27 ff.) has argued that the song in Isa. xlii. 10 ff. is a glossator's addition
to the text of Deutero-Isaiah.

[4] Isa. xii. 4 ff. Kissane (*op. cit.*, i, p. 147) holds that, 'assuming that Isaiah fore-
told the exile and the restoration, there is nothing in the poem which is not consistent with Isaian origin'. Most, however, including some whom Kissane char-
acterizes as 'usually conservative', regard the passage as late. Feldmann (*Das Buch
Isaias*, i, 1925, p. 164) is more than doubtful of its Isaianic authorship.

[5] Isa. xii. 5.

the heavens are higher than the earth, so are my ways higher than your ways, and my thoughts than your thoughts.'[1]

In treating of the Chinese teachers as statesmen and reformers, we found they were worthy to stand beside the Israelite prophets. Looked at in the setting of their own times and allowing for their different ways of expressing themselves, we may see in them deep moral earnestness and a burning desire to lead men into a finer world. In relation to worship, however, the prophets of Israel and the Sages of China are in two different worlds. It is not merely a question of the setting of their times. It is a question of the conception of worship. Some superficial points of similarity that may be found yield to a more fundamental divergence on closer examination. The prophets of Israel desired to make the ritual of worship more meaningful, and not merely more correct. It was not propriety but the spirit that concerned them. And they wanted to carry the spirit from the shrine into life and to make the service of God in daily life a part of the worship they sought to promote. The reason for this contrast is not far to seek, and to it we shall come in our final study.

[1] Isa. lv. 6 ff.

VI

The Prophet and God

A T the end of the previous lecture I said that in relation to worship the prophets of Israel and the three Chinese teachers who have engaged our attention lived in two different worlds. This was due to a fundamental difference in their conception of God and attitude to Him. To this difference I have frequently alluded in passing, but it now claims our more particular attention. In the first lecture the prophet was defined as one who delivers a message which is given to him. In a passage in Exodus we read: 'I have made thee a god to Pharaoh; and Aaron thy brother shall be thy prophet',[1] while elsewhere in the same book we find: 'Thou shalt speak unto him (i.e. unto Aaron), and put the words in his mouth. . . . And he shall be thy spokesman unto the people.[2] Again, in the story of the call of Jeremiah we read: 'Behold, I have put my words in thy mouth.'[3] In the account of several of the prophets of Israel we have the record of the call which came to them in some numinous experience. In the case of the Chinese teachers we have no similar record, and so far as we know, they did not have the same deep and immediate sense of God's presence in the moment of their consecration to their mission which the Israelite prophets had. Nevertheless, I have not denied them the name of prophet, but have recognized that they were charged with a genuine message from God.

Legge declares that Confucius was 'unreligious', and says that he deliberately chooses this term, rather than 'irreligious'.[4] How

---

[1] Exod. vii. 1.　　　　　[2] Exod. iv. 15 f.　　　　　[3] Jer. i. 9.

[4] The Chinese Classics, i, 2nd ed., p. 99. It is curious to note that in The Religions of China, 1880, pp. 10 f., Legge says: 'T'ien has had much of the force of the name Jahve, as explained by God Himself to Moses.' H. A. Giles (Confucianism and its

far I am prepared to accept this will become clear as we proceed. At the outset, however, I must disagree with one piece of evidence on which Legge relies. He says he thinks Confucius fell short of the older sages in his doctrine of God, since he prefers to speak of *Heaven* instead of the more personal *Ti* or *Shang Ti* of the older books.[1] This seems to me less than fair. It is well known that by New Testament times the Jews were unwilling to pronounce the divine name, but substituted some expression, such as 'the Name', or 'the Place', or 'Heaven', for it. In reading their Scriptures they used 'the Lord', and this passed over into the Greek, and was employed in the early Christian versions of the Bible, and this is found in most modern versions. Even the word 'God' was frequently not pronounced, and many modern Jews will not pronounce or write, save in a modified form, the Hebrew word for God, and in English prefer to write 'G–d'. This is not the mark of their 'unreligion', but of their extreme veneration for God. It is well known that the author of the Gospel of St. Matthew reflects this attitude to the extent of writing 'Kingdom of Heaven' instead of 'Kingdom of God', which we find in the parallel passages in the other Gospels. We do not label him as 'unreligious' on this ground.[2] Moreover, even in the older Chinese books, to which Legge refers, *Heaven* is found alongside *Shang Ti* or *Ti*, and it is clear that Heaven is conceived of in personal terms.[3] A single instance will here suffice. In the Great Declaration of King Wu,

Rivals, 1915, p. 12) says: 'A longer and closer acquaintance with the Confucian Canon has satisfied me that the proper equivalent of our word "God" is *T'ien*.' W. E. Soothill (*The Three Religions of China*, 3rd ed., 1929, p. 129) says: 'I do not find any evidence of the worship of Shang Ti by the people. In all the records with which I am acquainted He is worshipped only by the Supreme Ruler on earth. It is only in the impersonal or more general form of Heaven . . . that the people approach Him.'

[1] *Ibid.*, p. 98.

[2] On the use of *T'ien* cf. Waley, *The Analects of Confucius*, pp. 41 ff.

[3] E. R. Hughes (*The Great Learning and the Mean in Action*, p. 118) says: 'What the relation of *Shang Ti* to *T'ien* was in classical times . . . is one of the most difficult problems in Chinese studies. All I dare commit myself to here is that when using *Shang Ti* writers, on the whole, speak more anthropomorphically and anthropopathically than when using *T'ien*.'

after the recital of the iniquities of Chou we read 'Great Heaven was moved with indignation.'[1]

In one passage in the *Doctrine of the Mean* we find *Shang Ti* on the lips of Confucius,[2] where he says that King Wu and the Duke of Chou served Shang Ti by the ceremonies of the sacrifices to Heaven and Earth, but we can hardly use this passage with any confidence. Once in the *Analects* we find *Ti*,[3] but this is in the quotation of a saying attributed to T'ang,[4] and it offers no evidence of the usage of Confucius himself. In the Commentary on the *Great Learning* we find *Shang Ti* once[5] in a quotation from the *Shih Ching*.[6] None of these passages offers any serious evidence to offset the regular use of *T'ien*, or *Heaven*, by Confucius, and it is most probable that he deliberately chose this term.

We are told that 'the subjects on which the Master did not talk were: extraordinary things, feats of strength, disorder, and spiritual beings',[7] and that he advised his disciples to give themselves earnestly to their duties to men, but to keep aloof from spiritual beings, while respecting them.[8] This cannot be held to imply any doubt on the part of the Sage as to the reality of the existence of God, or of other spiritual beings. Such intimacy with God as the prophets of Israel knew was unthinkable to Confucius, because it would have offended his whole sense of propriety. It is recorded that he maintained a distant reserve towards his own son.[9] His whole idea of human relations was monarchic, each of the grades of society from the emperor downwards observing an

---

[1] *Shu Ching* V Book 1, Part 1, 5.   [2] *Doctrine of the Mean* xix. 6.

[3] *Analects* XX, i. 3.

[4] The quotation is based on *Shu Ching* IV Book 3, ii. 4, iii. 8. In iii. 8 the text of the *Shu Ching* has *Shang Ti*.

[5] *Great Learning*, Commentary x. 5.

[6] The quotation is from *Shih Ching* III Book 1, i. 6, with slight modification. For the *Shih Ching* cf. Legge, *The Chinese Classics*, iv, 2 vols, 1871, and B. Karlgren, *The Book of Odes*, 1950, for text and English translation. The Chinese text and French and Latin translations may be found in S. Couvreur, *Cheu King*, 3rd ed., 1934, and English translation without the Chinese text in A. Waley, *The Book of Songs*, 1937.

[7] *Analects* VII, xx.   [8] *Analects* VI, xx.

[9] *Analects* XVI , xiii. 5. Cf. Waley's note in *The Analects of Confucius*, p. 208 n., where it is said that 'there is a definite ritual severance between father and son'.

attitude of extreme deference to those above and reserve towards those below. It was this same attitude of distant deference which he maintained towards Heaven, and he would have regarded anything more intimate as shocking irreverence.[1] His wide difference from the Hebrew prophets may be recognized, but it is not fair to characterize as 'unreligious' an attitude consistent with profound awe and reverence merely because it was different from theirs. We may hold—as I hold—that it was far inferior in religious worth to their attitude, but it cannot be denied the name of religion.

I have more than once in these lectures cited Confucius's saying 'He who offends against Heaven has none to whom he can pray.'[2] This would seem to show that he thought of Heaven in personal terms. So, too, when he asks 'Is it not Heaven that knows me?'[3] Heaven to Confucius was clearly cognitive and moral. He also conceived of Heaven in terms of conscious purpose. 'Heaven produced the virtue[4] that is in me,' he said; 'Huan T'ui—what can he do to me?'[5] According to Ssu-ma Ch'ien the background of this remark was that Confucius was observing ceremonies with his disciples under a tree in Sung, when Huan T'ui, an officer of the state, sought to kill him. The Sage withdrew, but without haste, Ssu-ma Ch'ien says, and made this remark which implies the conscious protection of Heaven of one upon whom the mandate of Heaven lay.[6]

On another occasion, immediately preceding the remark cited above 'Is it not Heaven that knows me?', he said 'I do not murmur against Heaven; I do not grumble against men',[7] and in the

[1] Cf. C. Y. Hsu, *The Philosophy of Confucius*, 1926, p. 58: 'Instead of being indifferent towards divinity, his attitude is rather reserved.'

[2] *Analects* III, xiii. We may compare with this saying a saying of Mo-tzŭ's: 'He who sins against Heaven has no place to which he can flee' (xxviii, Mei, p. 151; Forke, p. 331; Tomkinson, p. 94).

[3] *Analects* XIV, xxxvii. The rendering given here is the literal rendering which stands in Legge's note and not the rendering of his text. Cf. the renderings of Couvreur and Pauthier. Waley has: 'perhaps after all I am known; not here, but in heaven'.   [4] Waley renders *tê* by *power*.   [5] *Analects* VII, xxii.

[6] *Shih Chi* xlvii (cf. Chavannes, *Les Mémoires historiques*, v, pp. 336 f.; Wilhelm, *Confucius and Confucianism*, p. 29).   [7] *Analects* XIV, xxxvii.

Doctrine of the Mean his teaching is reflected in the observation: 'The superior man is quiet and calm, waiting for the appointments of Heaven.'[1] This may be represented as a form of fatalism, and one of Mo-tzŭ's strongest criticisms against Confucianism was its fatalism.[2] But while it might become fatalism when a blind and impersonal power is substituted for a personal God, it is worthy of some higher name if it is confidence that the man who is given a divinely appointed task, and who in obedience to the mandate of Heaven seeks to carry out that task, need have no fear of men, who are powerless to frustrate Heaven's purpose.[3]

That Confucius believed that he had a divinely appointed task is especially clear from one passage, which relates that he was once in peril in K'uang. His calmness was unruffled, and he simply observed that the cause of truth[4] had been entrusted to him by Heaven, and that it could not be the purpose of Heaven that it should perish. What could the men of K'uang do to him?[5] His confidence in the power of Heaven to preserve him, and his sense of a mission to men appointed by Heaven, is as strong as that of the prophets of Israel. Where he falls short of them is in the remoteness of God, and in the littleness of the place that God had in his teaching.[6] While for him God was real and His purpose clear, his unwillingness to talk about Him meant that he did little to make Him

---

[1] *Doctrine of the Mean* xiv. 4.

[2] *Mo-tzŭ* xxxix (Mei, p. 202; Forke, pp. 398 f.; Tomkinson, p. 161). To one of Confucius's disciples fatalism is attributed in one of the stories recorded in Ssu-ma Ch'ien's *Shih Chi*. There it is said that the Master was arrested in P'u, whereupon Kung Liang-ju observed: 'When I formerly joined the Master, we met with difficulties in K'uang. Today we again meet with difficulties here. That is fate. I will fight and die rather than again see the Master caught in difficulties' (xlvii, translation of Wilhelm, *Confucius and Confucianism*, E.Tr., p. 32; cf. Chavannes, *Les Mémoires historiques*, v, p. 345).

[3] On the fatalism of some Chinese schools cf. my *Submission in Suffering*, pp. 36 ff.

[4] Cf. above, p. 5 n.   [5] *Analects* IX, v.

[6] Cf. L. Giles (*The Sayings of Confucius*, p. 25): 'Religion was a subject which he disliked to discuss and certainly did not profess to teach. . . . And the reason why he refrained from descanting on such matters was that, knowing nothing of them himself, he felt that he would have been guilty of hypocrisy and fraud had he made a show of instructing others therein.'

real for his followers. There might be a will of God for him, but he said nothing to make men feel that there was a will of God for them, and worship was but the offering of reverence and not the receiving of grace. Hence, in effect his teaching was reduced to ethics, instead of the communication of the religion which he himself had.[1]

Of Mencius it is not necessary to say much. Once we find the expression *Shang Ti* on his lips,[2] in addition to two citations which contain it. Of these one was from the *Shih Ching* and the other from the *Shu Ching*.[3] Elsewhere he speaks of *Heaven*, which seems to have been even more remote to him than to Confucius. Nevertheless he seems to have conceived of Heaven in personal terms,[4] even though in remote and rather colourless terms. He says: 'When Heaven is about to confer a great office on any man, it first exercises his mind with suffering, and his sinews and bones with toil. It exposes his body to hunger, and subjects him to extreme poverty. It confounds his undertakings. By all these methods it stimulates his mind, hardens his nature, and supplies his incompetencies.'[5] But this is a meagre basis on which to erect any vital religious faith. Mencius was conscious of a mission to check the doctrines of Yang Chu and Mo-tzŭ and to defend the principles of Confucius, and to rectify the ills of his time,[6] but

[1] Cf. E. D. Edwards, *Confucius*, p. 4: 'He (i.e. Confucius) was concerned, not with religion but with ethics, and aimed not at the salvation of the soul, but at the restoration of order in society and the state.' With this cf. what I. G. Matthews (*The Religious Pilgrimage of Israel*, 1947, p. 128) says of the pre-exilic prophets of Israel: 'These men had denounced ritual as of no avail, but now, if possible, they went farther, and made social ethics the essential, even the sole, requirements of Yahweh.'

[2] *Mencius* IV Part 2, xxv. 2.

[3] *Mencius* I Part 2, iii. 7 (cited from *Shu Ching* V Book 1, Part 1, 7, with some modifications), IV Part 1, vii. 5 (cited from *Shih Ching* III Book 1, i. 4).

[4] L. Giles (*The Book of Mencius*, 1942, p. 15) complains that translators have heightened the impression of Mencius's silence about religion by fighting shy of the rendering God for *T'ien*. Cf. also H. A. Giles, *Confucianism and its Rivals*, pp. 89 ff., where it is maintained that Mencius was essentially religious, and believed in a personal God. Against this cf. Forke, *Die Gedankenwelt des chinesischen Kulturkreises*, 1927, p. 43: 'Im übrigen lehnt Mêng-tse die Personifizierung des Himmels ab und gebraucht niemals den Ausdruck Gott.'

[5] *Mencius* VI Part 2, xv. 2.   [6] *Mencius* III Part 2, ix. 9.

perhaps it would be truer to say that the mantle of Confucius had
fallen upon him than that the mandate of Heaven had been given
to him. Mediately it was the mandate of Heaven, since the task
he had taken up from Confucius had been the mandate of Heaven,
but with Mencius, even more than with his predecessor, it was the
task more than the Giver of the task that occupied his attention.

That Mencius had no belief in a blind fate is shown by his
citation on two occasions[1] of a passage from the *Shu Ching*, which
says: 'Calamities sent by Heaven may be avoided, but from calamities brought on by oneself there is no escape.'[2] Again he said:
'Death sustained in the discharge of one's duties may correctly
be ascribed to the appointment of Heaven. Death under handcuffs
and fetters cannot be correctly so ascribed.'[3] To Mencius men live
in a moral universe, where evil brings its own reward. At the
same time there are inscrutable facts to be explained, since goodness is not always successful nor virtue always rewarded. Hence
Mencius turned to the will of God as a partial explanation of the
mysteries of experience, and not as the simple and sufficient
explanation of everything. Heaven was purposeful, if pale and
remote. How pale and remote is clear from a passage which
records his answer to the question whether Yao gave the throne
to Shun. Mencius replied that he did not, but that it was Heaven
which gave it to him. When asked how Heaven did this he replied
that Heaven does not speak, but that it was by the will of the
people that the will of Heaven was known.[4] Mencius finished by
quoting with approval a passage from the *Shu Ching*: 'Heaven
sees according as my people see; Heaven hears according as my
people hear.'[5] This amounts merely to the doctrine *Vox populi vox
Dei*, to which none of the Israelite prophets we have studied
would have subscribed.

Neither in Confucius nor in Mencius, therefore, do we find a
very rich or satisfying doctrine of God. In Mo-tzŭ, however, we

[1] *Mencius* II Part I, iv. 6, IV Part I, viii. 5.
[2] *Shu Ching* IV Book 5, Part 2, ii. 3 (also in *Li Chi* xxx. 16).
[3] *Mencius* VII Part I, ii. 3 f.
[4] *Mencius* V Part I, v.
[5] *Shu Ching* VI Book I, ii. 7.

find something far superior to either. His normal term for God is Heaven, as theirs was, and for Him Heaven was both personal and interested in men. There was a mandate of Heaven for every man, and when Mo-tzŭ speaks of the will of Heaven, it is not merely Heaven's will for the ruler or for himself, or for the state in general, but Heaven's will for individual men, who are called to make that will their rule of life through love for all around them.

Some writers have discounted this side of Mo-tzŭ's teaching, and have regarded it as merely a convenience, a buttress to support his utilitarianism, or a personification of his own principles. De Rosny thinks he was devoid of any idea of God,[1] and Mei observes that 'what Heaven desires is just what Motse has been teaching himself'.[2] This is a curious criticism, and it would seem to imply that Mo-tzŭ could have been pronounced more truly religious if he had summoned men to do what he believed to be opposed to the will of God. Every prophet who believes himself to be the spokesman of God summons men to do what he believes to be the will of God. This is true of Confucius and Mencius, but they were less interested in the common man, save as a sufferer from misgovernment, and so did not proclaim that will for ordinary men to the extent that Mo-tzŭ did.

He proclaimed with emphasis that Heaven desires righteousness,[3] and believed that in preaching righteousness he was doing the will of Heaven. Righteousness is the standard set for men by Heaven, and to be followed from the emperor down to the

---

[1] *Études de critique et d'histoire*, 1896, p. 299.

[2] *Motse, rival of Confucius*, p. 149. Cf. p. 158: 'He threw a religious halo around his fundamental ethical convictions.' So D. T. Suzuki (*Brief History of Early Chinese Philosophy*, 1914, p. 100) says that Mo-tzŭ 'conceded the first place to utilitarianism, for the execution of which the God idea became necessary to him'; S. Holth (*Micius*, 1935, p. 48) that 'his religious convictions were made to support his main interest in the ethical and social relations of life'; Alexandra David (*Le philosophe Meh-Ti*, 1907, p. 142) that 'génies, mânes ou l'empereur suprême (Chang-ti) ne jouent aucun rôle dans ces discours. Si l'on nous y propose l'imitation du Ciel . . . c'est uniquement pour nous donner un haut exemple . . . rien y trouver qui ressemble au commandement d'une Puissance supérieure.'

[3] *Mo-tzŭ* xxvi (Mei, p. 136; Forke, p. 315; Tomkinson, p. 84).

common people.[1] The will of Heaven, or righteousness, is as the compasses to the wheelwright, or the square to the carpenter.[2]

Moreover, Heaven rewards those who obey His will, from the emperor downwards. 'When the emperor practises virtue,' he says, 'Heaven rewards; when the emperor does evil Heaven punishes.'[3] Again, 'whoso obeys the will of Heaven, loving universally and benefiting others, will obtain rewards, while whoso resists the will of Heaven, by being partial and harming others, will incur punishment'.[4] A Heaven that is morally discriminating is surely conceived in personal terms.[5] The prophets of Israel promised disasters and divine discipline when men did evil, and it is hard not to find that Mo-tzŭ stands alongside them. 'For the murder of an innocent man,' he said, 'there will be a calamity.'[6] When Naboth had been judicially murdered at Jezebel's instigation, Elijah was sent to say to Ahab 'In the place where dogs licked the blood of Naboth shall dogs lick thy blood.'[7] Elijah announced this word in personal terms to the man who profited by Naboth's murder, while Mo-tzŭ announced the principle in general terms. But the message is fundamentally one.

It is of interest, too, to notice that Mo-tzŭ traces this discipline of Heaven to the love of Heaven. He says that Heaven loves the whole world, and proves that love by visiting with calamity those who sin against their fellows.[8] We hail the profound insight of Amos for linking the love of God with His discipline of Israel, when he said 'You only have I known of all the families of the earth; therefore will I visit your iniquities upon you.'[9] Yet here

[1] *Mo-tzŭ* xxvi (Mei, p. 136; Forke, p. 316; Tomkinson, p. 85).
[2] *Mo-tzŭ* xxvi (Mei, p. 140; Forke, p. 320; Tominson, p. 87).
[3] *Mo-tzŭ* xxvii (Mei, p. 141; Forke, p. 321; Tomkinson, p. 88).
[4] *Mo-tzŭ* xxvi (Mei, p. 137; Forke, p. 317; Tomkinson, p. 86).
[5] Cf. Forke, *Geschichte der alten chinesischen Philosophie*, p. 377: 'Der Himmel ist für Mê Ti . . . ein anthropomorphes Wesen, das wie ein potenzierter Mensch erscheint, denn er hat menschliche Leidenschaften, er liebt die Guten und hasst die Bösen, erkennt, was in der Welt vorgeht und regiert sie danach.' Cf. also *Die Gedankenwelt des chinesischen Kulturkreises*, 1927, p. 43.
[6] *Mo-tzŭ* xxvi (Mei, p. 139; Forke, p. 319; Tomkinson, p. 87).
[7] 1 Kings xxi. 19.
[8] *Mo-tzŭ* xxviii (Mei, p. 154; Forke, p. 334; Tomkinson, p. 96).
[9] Amos iii. 2.

Mo-tzŭ has a similar insight. A Heaven that loves men is surely personal. Williamson says 'The "will of Heaven" was to him the ultimate and universal standard, by which everything was to be judged. His interpretation of the will of Heaven is of peculiar interest, in that, according to modern critics like Liang Ch'i Ch'ao and Hu Shih, it permits of a personal interpretation. In fact, it would seem that the personal interpretation is the only one which meets the case.'[1]

'What is the will of Heaven that is to be obeyed?' asks Mo-tzŭ. 'It is to love all the people in the world universally.'[2] We regard it as part of the peculiar glory of Israel's prophets that they taught that what God is perceived to be they who worship Him must seek to become, so far as may be under human conditions. Yet Mo-tzŭ has the same principle. Heaven exemplifies an all-embracing love for men, and so the will of Heaven for men is that they should manifest a similar love for one another. I find it hard to see why Mo-tzŭ should be dismissed as fundamentally irreligious, and as a mere personifier of his own teachings and projector of this personification as a buttress for his teachings.

His opposition to aggressive war is similarly based on the will of Heaven. Man's highest good is what Heaven wills for him. One modern writer has noted that Mo-tzŭ's Heaven is interested in men, and concludes that he seems to have conceived of Heaven as a person, though he nowhere refers to Him in personalistic terms.[3] I find it hard to see how he can be said not to have used personalistic terms. It is true that he does not use the anthropomorphic language with which we are familiar in the Old Testament. He does not speak of the hand of God, or the heart of God. But these are only metaphors, of rich psychological value indeed,

---

[1] Mo Ti, p. 35. Other scholars who have maintained that Mo-tzŭ's Heaven was personal are Wilhelm, Die chinesischen Literatur, 1926, p. 57, and A Short History of Chinese Civilization, E.Tr., 1929, p. 151; Forke, Mê Ti, p. 40; F. E. A. Krause, Ju-Tao-Fo, 1924, p. 89; H. Hackmann, Chinesische Philosophie, 1927, p. 111. J. Witte (Mê Ti, 1928, p. 11) holds that Mo-tzŭ was a pantheist (against this cf. W. Eberhard, in A.R.W., xxxiii, 1936, p. 316), while W. Corswant (R.Th.Ph., N.S. xxxiv, 1946, p. 116) thinks he was a Deist.

[2] Mo-tzŭ xxviii (Mei, p. 153; Forke, p. 333; Tomkinson, p. 95).

[3] Cf. F. Rawlinson, The Chinese Recorder, lxiii, 1932, p. 95.

but not theologically significant. Since Mo-tzŭ conceives of Heaven as loving men, as interested in men, as having a moral purpose for men, as governing the world by moral principles, as setting demands for men by exemplifying the qualities demanded, he cannot be said to have thought of Heaven as a pale abstraction.

I have already said that Mo-tzŭ opposed the fatalistic strain in Confucianism, though I have also said[1] that Confucius and Mencius could only be said to have taught fatalism with the strongest reservations.[2] It would be easy to cull texts from the Old Testament which seem to teach that what happens must happen,[3] but it would be very untrue to the teaching of the Old Testament as a whole. Jeremiah felt himself driven by an irresistible compulsion to prophesy against his own will, and roundly asserted that God had seduced him. 'I am become a laughing-stock all the day,' he said, 'every one mocketh me. For as often as I speak, I cry out; I cry, Violence and spoil: because the word of the Lord is made a reproach unto me, and a derision all the day. And if I say, I will

[1] Cf. what I have said in *Submission in Suffering*, pp. 35 ff. In Ssŭ-ma Ch'ien's *Shih Chi*, it is recorded how Confucius was once induced to visit Nan-tzŭ, the notorious wife of the Duke of Wei, and when Tzŭ Lu was displeased the Sage excused himself by saying 'Whatever I have done wrong, Heaven forced me to do it, Heaven forced me to do it' (xlvii, translation of Wilhelm, *Confucius and Confucianism*, E.Tr., p. 28; cf. Chavannes, *Les Mémoires historiques*, v, p. 335). At the most this could be pressed to mean no more than 'Circumstances forced me.' In *Analects* VI, xxvi, where the incident is more briefly referred to, Legge renders the saying 'Wherein I have done imperfectly may Heaven reject me! May Heaven reject me!' Waley renders 'Whatsoever I have done amiss, may Heaven avert it, may Heaven avert it!' and says (p. 255) that the character in the text is an abbreviation for another. H. A. Giles (*Confucianism and its Rivals*, 1915, p. 71) renders it 'If I have done anything wrong, may God strike me dead, may God strike me dead', while L. Giles (*The Sayings of Confucius*, p. 84) renders 'In whatsoever I have sinned, may I be abominable in the sight of God!' On so differently interpreted a passage it is impossible to establish any really deterministic view on the part of Confucius.

[2] Cf. Fung Yu-lan, *The Spirit of Chinese Philosophy*, E.Tr., p. 34: 'The idea of fate which the Mohists denounced was not what the Confucianists held.'

[3] The Old Testament nowhere expresses any belief in a blind Fate, but there are passages which would seem to suggest that men are the puppets of God. Cf. Gen. xlv. 8: 'It was not you that sent me hither, but God'; Exod. ix. 12: 'The Lord hardened the heart of Pharaoh'; Isa. v. 18, x. 5; Jer. i. 5; Amos vii. 14.

not make mention of him, nor speak any more in his name, then there is in mine heart as it were a burning fire shut up in my bones, and I am weary with forbearing, and I cannot contain.'¹ It matters not whether we speak of God, or of Heaven, or of Fate. If the life and lot of men are irrevocably appointed for them, and they are as completely helpless as they sometimes feel themselves to be, and if man is denied moral freedom and subject to a rigid determinism, then all prophecy is in vain, and it is futile to attempt to alter what cannot be altered. Neither Confucius nor Mencius were really thoroughgoing fatalists, though one might suppose from Mo-tzŭ's denunciations that Confucianism was essentially fatalistic.² He declares that the Confucianist holds tenaciously to the dogma of fate, and takes it to be the basic principle of life.³ He himself declares that the belief in fatalism is the greatest evil in the world, and that it undermines resolution and effort.⁴ He denounces it as the invention of tyrants, and the practice of miserable men.⁵ 'Fatalism', he says, 'is not helpful to Heaven above, nor to the spirits of the middle sphere, nor to man below. The eccentric belief in this doctrine is responsible for pernicious ideas and is the way of the wicked.'⁶

Of the Chinese teachers with whom we have been concerned Mo-tzŭ stands the highest. His teaching is more intimately associated with religion than either that of Confucius or that of Mencius. Wieger says he is the only Chinese of whom it can be thought that he believed in God.⁷ That this goes too far I have

---

¹ Jer. xx. 7 ff.

² *Mo-tzŭ* xxxix (Mei, p. 202; Forke, pp. 389 f.; Tomkinson, p. 161). For Mo-tzŭ's opposition to fatalism cf. also *Mo-tzŭ* xxxv-xxxvii.

³ *Mo-tzŭ* xxxix (Mei, p. 202; Forke, pp. 398 f.; Tomkinson, p. 161).

⁴ *Mo-tzŭ* xxxv (Mei, pp. 187 f.; Forke, p. 382; Tomkinson, pp. 114 f.).

⁵ *Mo-tzŭ* xxxvii (Mei, p. 199; Forke, p. 395; Tomkinson, p. 122).

⁶ *Mo-tzŭ* xxxv (Mei, p. 188; Forke, p. 382; Tomkinson, pp. 114 f.).

⁷ *Histoire des Croyances religieuses*, 2nd ed., p. 207. E. Faber (*Die Grundgedanken des alten chinesischen Sozialismus*, 1877, p. 27) thought of him as a forerunner of Christ, while Liang Ch'i-ch'ao (*History of Chinese Political Thought*, 1930, p. 110) observed that 'he evolved a religious system very similar to Christianity'. Hoang Tsen-yue (*Étude comparative sur les philosophies de Lao Tseu, Khong Tseu, Mo Tseu*, 1925, p. 143) declared that the doctrine of Mo-tzŭ and Christianity were as twin sisters. Against such an idea S. Cognetti de Martiis (in *Memorie della R. Accademia*

already indicated, but the statement of Hu Shih that he was the only Chinese who can be said to have founded a religion is truer.[1] Confucius believed in God, but he does not seem to have contributed to any new or richer understanding of the character and will of God. But Mo-tzŭ did bring a new fullness of content to the idea of God, and did unfold new ideas on His character and will. Where he fails is in that he does not call men into any direct relationship with this God. He teaches that Heaven loves men and wills that men should love one another; but he does not call men to love Heaven. He proclaims the will of Heaven, but he offers men no source of power in worship and fellowship for the fulfilment of that will. Worship to him was still but reverence, something that man brought to God, rather than the meeting of man with God, whereby grace and power were mediated to him.

It is precisely here that the strength of the prophets of Israel lay. To them God was unquestionably real and personal. The very abundance of the anthropomorphic language which they use puts this beyond all doubt. They came to men with a vigorous 'Thus saith the Lord.' Again and again they closed their oracles by saying 'This is the very word of the Lord.' They do not speak only of God in the third person as the Chinese Sages did. God's word is couched in the first person very frequently. The prophet felt himself to be so much the mouthpiece or messenger of God that he could pass over from speaking of Him in the third person to speaking in the first person, as though God himself were uttering the word.[2] It was the word of God in his mouth, spoken with all the authority of God.

It follows from this that God is not thought of as remote, seen

dei Lincei, 4th series, Classe de Scienze morali, iii, 1887, p. 261) objects that the similarities are extrinsic, and that the spirit is widely different.

[1] The Development of the Logical Method in Ancient China, 1928, p. 57.

[2] Cf. A. R. Johnson, The One and the Many in the Israelite Conception of God, 1942, pp. 36 ff. Cf. also G. Hölscher, Die Profeten, 1914, p. 25: 'Die Profeten reden nicht nur im Auftrage und nach dem Geheisse Jahwes, wiederholen nicht nur Worte und Offenbarungen, die der Gott ihnen zugeraunt oder in der Vision gezeigt hat, sondern sie reden als Gott selbst und identifizieren sich, solange sie ekstatisch sprechen, durchaus mit ihm.'

only though the mists of incense, and worshipped by men who lift their eyes to Him from afar. He is close to men. 'Their God is not the remote,' says R. B. Y. Scott, 'dispassionate, abstract deity who becomes a term of abstract discussion. The God we meet in the pages of Amos, Isaiah and Jeremiah can only be described as a vigorous and vivid personality, majestic indeed, and divinely "other" than man, and yet meeting him in the commerce of mind with mind and of will with will.'[1] In the book of Isaiah we have the familiar word 'Come now and let us reason together.'[2] Here we have a God Who is not only interested in men, and Who not only declares His will to men, but Who draws near to them. He may discipline them, as the prophets so frequently declared that He would; but He also seeks them pleads and with them. 'O my people, what have I done unto thee? And wherein have I wearied thee?'[3] He calls men not alone that they may offer their defence of their ways, and be convicted by His reproaches, but that they may know Him with an immediacy of knowledge comparable with that which the prophet himself enjoys. 'Let not the wise man glory in his wisdom, neither let the mighty man glory in his might, let not the rich man glory in his riches; but let him that glorieth glory in this, that he understandeth and knoweth me.'[4]

Each of the prophets emphasized particular aspects of the character of God, but all called men to reflect in their lives the same essential character. It was by what He was, no less than by His word, that He summoned them to the way of His will. His love for men is proclaimed no less clearly here than by Mo-tzŭ, and with a tenderness Mo-tzŭ did not know. 'When Israel was a child, then I loved him, and called my son out of Egypt.'[5] Even in her waywardness and disobedience she was pursued by His love, and the succession of prophets whom He raised up to call her back to Himself were the evidence of that love. More moving

---

[1] *The Relevance of the Prophets*, 1944, p. 211.

[2] Isa. i. 18. The Hebrew word is sometimes understood forensically to mean 'let us go to law with one another'; alternatively it may mean 'let us argue with one another', or 'have things out with one another'.

[3] Mic. vi. 3.   [4] Jer. ix. 23 f.   [5] Hos. xi. 1.

still is the cry of Hosea in the name of God: 'How shall I give thee up, Ephraim? How shall I deliver thee, Israel? . . . Mine heart is turned within me, my compassions are kindled together.'[1]

It is frequently said that Amos emphasizes the demand of God for righteousness, and Hosea the love of God and its corollary in demand upon men, and Isaiah the holiness of God as a consuming flame, that must either consume all that is unholy and transmute into its own purity whoever comes into His presence, or must destroy the sinner with his sin. None of these represents the exclusive message of any of these prophets. Amos is aware of the love of God, and Isaiah calls for justice. For God is inflexibly just in their thought, and His justice is one of the expressions of His love. It is not the only expression. But the prophets perceived that a God Who was indifferent to all the injustice and oppression that was rampant in Israel could not really love men.

To the prophets of Israel God was in final control of history. He was not merely a spectator of human activity instructing them through the prophets as to how they should act and watching their follies and their mistakes with concern, but Himself an actor on the stage of history. Sometimes there is the appeal to the great acts of deliverance of the past, and sometimes the assurance that He is in the events of the present. It is never suggested that He is responsible for everything that happens, or that human wills are unreal. No prophet appeals more to the past than Deutero-Isaiah. But his appeal to the past is the basis of his confidence for the future.[2] The God Who led Israel out of Egypt in the past will lead her from Babylon to her own land, and will break the power of the Chaldaean oppressor as easily as He broke the power of the Egyptian.[3]

Long before Deutero-Isaiah's day, Amos had expressed the same faith that God was in final control of history. The migrations of the peoples were controlled by Him. Not only had He brought

[1] Hos. xi. 8.

[2] Cf. C. R. North, in *Studies in Old Testament Prophecy* (T. H. Robinson Festschrift, ed. by H. H. Rowley), 1950, pp. 111 ff., and A. Bentzen, in *Studia Theologica*, i, 1948, pp. 183 ff.

[3] Isa. xlii. 10 ff., xliii. 19 ff., xlviii. 14, li. 9 ff., lii. 9 ff.

the Israelites from Egypt. The Philistines and the Aramaeans were also watched over by Him, and their migration to their present homes had been directed by Him.[1] God's interest was not limited to Israel, and neither was His discipline. For their transgressions against morality and for their cruel oppressions He would visit the neighbours of Israel, no less than Israel herself.[2] Isaiah could picture Him whistling for the peoples from afar to come to do His will,[3] and integrating into His own purpose the purposes of their hearts, even though they were themselves evil purposes, for which they stood condemned before Him.[4]

The Chinese Sages also believed that God was active in history, indeed. In calamities and rebellions, and in the punishment of evil deeds, they saw the evidence of His hand, though in a more impersonal and remote way than the Israelite prophets.

Nor was history alone under His control. Nature lay in the hollow of His hand. 'Seek him that made the Pleiades and Orion,' says Amos, 'that turneth the darkness into the morning, and maketh the day dark with night; that calleth for the waters of the sea, and poureth them out upon the face of the earth; Yahweh is his name.'[5] Or again Jeremiah says: 'He hath made the earth by his power, he hath established the world by his wisdom, and by his understanding hath he stretched out the heavens: when he uttereth his voice, there is a tumult of waters in the heavens, and he causeth the vapours to ascend from the ends of the earth; he maketh lightnings for the rain, and bringeth forth the wind out of his treasuries.'[6] Deutero-Isaiah in familiar words says: 'Who hath measured the waters in the hollow of his hand, and meted out the heaven with the span, and comprehended the dust of the earth in a measure, and weighed the mountains in scales, and the hills in a balance? . . . It is he that sitteth upon the circle of the earth, and the inhabitants thereof are as grasshoppers; that stretcheth out the heavens as a curtain, and spreadeth them out as a tent

[1] Amos ix. 7.   [2] Amos i. 3 ff., 6 ff., 9 f., 11 f., 13 ff., ii. 1 ff.
[3] Isa. vii. 18.   [4] Isa. x. 5 ff.
[5] Amos v. 8.   [6] Jer. li. 15 f.

to dwell in.'[1] Here again, while there is nothing to match the brilliance of some of these passages in Confucius, or Mencius, or Mo-tzǔ—and the undistinguished style of Mo-tzǔ has been noted by Chinese authors[2]—from what I have said it is clear that the Chinese teachers thought of Heaven as controlling natural powers. He could bring natural calamities of flood and drought upon men in token of His displeasure. The difference between Israelite and Chinese teachers here must not be exaggerated therefore. The more richly personal character of the Biblical thought of God and the magnificent literary style of some of the familiar passages may be recognized, but in the thought of the Chinese teachers the power of God was not less recognized.

In speaking of worship I emphasized the Hebrew prophetic conception of it as communion, and not merely as the offering of reverence and homage, and I have more than once referred to the two-way traffic of worship in their thought. It became the medium of grace for man's enrichment, as they conceived it; and this was because of their conception of the Being of God. His love for men is not displayed merely in the remote showering of blessings upon them, but in His transforming touch upon men. On the day when he received his inaugural vision the Isaiah who entered the Temple was not the Isaiah who came away. The very springs of his being had been cleansed and renewed as he stood before God. The prophetic condemnation of so much of the worship of their day was just that it had not this effect. There was no true fellowship between man and God, whereby the cleansing power of God might be felt.

In the thought of the prophets of Israel, God is not merely a demanding God, Who lays His law upon men, and requires their obedience. He is a God Who offers strength for the fulfilment of

---

[1] Isa. xl. 12 ff.

[2] Cf. *Han-Fei-tzǔ* xxxii (a passage not translated in W. K. Liao, *The Complete Works of Han Fei Tzǔ*, i, 1939, which only reaches chapter xxx). The passage is translated in my *Submission in Suffering*, p. 115. Cf. also Waley, *Three Ways of Thought in Ancient China*, 1939, pp. 163 f.: 'Mo Tzu is feeble, repetitive, heavy, unimaginative and unentertaining, devoid of a single passage that could possibly be said to have wit, beauty or force.'

His demands; He is a God Who forgives the iniquities of men who appear before Him in penitence, and Who renews their spirits within them. 'Though your sins be as scarlet, they shall be as white as snow; though they be red like crimson, they shall be as wool.'[1] 'Come and let us return unto the Lord: for he hath torn and he will heal us; he hath smitten and he will bind us up.'[2] No element of this thought of God as pleading with men and as ready to forgive and renew is to be found in the Chinese teachers. To them He is the emperor, whereas to the Hebrews He could be thought of as the husband of His people. 'I will betroth thee unto me for ever; yea I will betroth thee unto me in righteousness, and in judgement, and in loving kindness, and in mercies. I will even betroth thee unto me in faithfulness: and thou shalt know the Lord.'[3] 'Where is the bill of your mother's divorcement, where-with I have put her away?'[4]

It is hard to think of any of the Chinese teachers using the language of divine comfort that we find in Deutero-Isaiah. 'Comfort ye, comfort ye my people, saith your God. Speak ye comfortably to Jerusalem, and cry unto her, that her warfare is accomplished, that her iniquity is pardoned; that she hath received of the Lord's hand double for all her sins.'[5] 'Fear thou not, for I am with thee; yea, I will uphold thee with the right hand of my righteousness.'[6] 'When thou passest through the waters, I will be with thee; and through the rivers they shall not overflow thee: when thou walkest through the fire, thou shalt not be burned; neither shall the flame kindle upon thee.'[7] 'Break forth into joy, sing together, ye waste places of Jerusalem: for the Lord hath comforted his people, he hath redeemed Jerusalem.'[8]

It is in this conception of the more intimate relationship between God and men that the religion of the prophets is most sharply to be distinguished from that of the Chinese teachers. While I would credit them with a conception of Heaven as personal, as against

---

[1] Isa. i. 18.
[2] Hos. vi. 1.
[3] Hos. ii. 19 f.
[4] Isa. l. 1.
[5] Isa. xl. 1 f.
[6] Isa. xli. 10.
[7] Isa. xlii. 2.
[8] Isa. lii. 9.

some of their critics, and believe that they felt that they were charged with a mission by Heaven, I would differentiate them from the great prophets of Israel by their sense of the remoteness of Him whom they served, and their consequent inability to make Him real for their followers. This is not to depreciate them or to use them merely to set off the glory of the Israelite prophets. The sense of God as richly personal goes back farther than the eighth-century prophets. They enjoyed a heritage which was not given to Confucius. In the ancient traditions which were given literary form before the eighth century there are stories of the patriarchs, which tell how they saw God face to face and spoke to Him. How far these were read literally in the time of the prophets we may not know. But they certainly fostered the thought of God as near, and as entering into intimate relations with men. There was also the story of the Exodus from Egypt, telling how God chose Israel in her weakness and affliction, and sent Moses to lead her forth. If I may be pardoned the expression without being misunderstood, God seemed to Israel to be so intensely human while yet being so far removed from man. He was human in sympathy and in love, human in His means of approach to man, yet far removed from man in His power and His holiness and His majesty. But with Israel majesty did not mean unapproachableness. It demanded reverence and awe; but with it could go nearness.

It is also necessary that we should remember that the prophets of Israel had in the experience of their call something which was not given to the Chinese teachers, so far as we know. This very experience helped to give them that sense of the nearness of God and to develop in their thought of God that element that is lacking in the sages of China. When Amos was pursuing his ordinary avocation he felt a constraint laid upon him to go to Israel to prophesy,[1] a constraint which was as irresistible as that fire burning in Jeremiah's bones.[2] He could no more resist that constraint than one could resist the catch at the heart on hearing the roar of the lion at large. He associated that constraint with God, Who thus seemed

[1] Amos vii. 15.   [2] Jer. xx. 9.

to come near to him and to claim him forcibly for His service. 'The lion hath roared, who will not fear? The Lord God hath spoken, who can but prophesy?'[1] He describes his sense of the intimacy with God granted to him by saying 'Surely the Lord God will do nothing, but he revealeth his secret unto his servants the prophets.'[2] To Hosea there came an irresistible constraint which he expresses as the command of God to take 'a wife of whoredom'.[3] This is understood by some to mean that he felt driven to marry a temple prostitute,[4] and it seems to me a probable, though not a certain, view. Hosea loathed the fertility cult and all its ways, and if this view is correct he felt constrained to do what must have seemed to him most revolting.[5] The strength of the constraint laid upon him is then seen the more clearly, and he believed this was the constraint of God. Little wonder that God seemed real and near and personal to him. It was only subsequently that out of the agony of his own experience and his deep love for the woman who so ill requited his love that he came to perceive the greatness of God's love for Israel. Of the experience of Isaiah in the moment of his call I have already spoken. The man who had that experience could not think of God in merely abstract terms or forget the sense of immediate access to His presence. To Jeremiah the call came when he was still a diffident youth, and he tried to fight against it.[6] But the constraint was too strong for him, and he felt that even before his birth he had been marked out for this service, and that God's claim on him could not be rejected.

Had Confucius or Mencius or Mo-tzŭ known this kind of experience there might have been that warmer and more intimate note in their religious teaching that we find in the Hebrew prophets. They are not to be depreciated because they did not know it; on the other hand the fact that they did not know it

---

[1] Amos iii. 8.   [2] Amos iii. 7.   [3] Hos. i. 2.

[4] So T. H. Robinson, in *T.S.K.*, cvi, 1934–5, pp. 301 ff., H. Schmidt, in *Z.A.W.*, N.F. i, 1924, pp. 245 ff., O. R. Sellers, in *A.J.S.L.*, xli, 1924–5, pp. 243 ff., H. G. May, in *J.B.L.*, lv, 1936, pp. 285 ff., W. A. Irwin, in J. M. P. Smith, *The Prophets and Their Times*, 2nd ed., 1941, pp. 71 f.

[5] Cf. A. Allwohn, *Die Ehe des Propheten Hosea*, 1926.

[6] Jer. i. 4 ff.

while Hebrew prophets did, and that in consequence the latter
stood on a higher plane of prophecy, is not to be obscured. The
objectivity of comparative study requires it to be underlined.

It is surprising to find how little is said in the prophets about
love for God. It has been said that love to God and love to man
are primary principles of Old Testament religion, as well as of
New Testament religion. When such love is inculcated in the New
Testament[1] it is supported by Old Testament texts from Deuteronomy[2] and Leviticus.[3] So far as the call for love for God in the
Old Testament is concerned, it is to be found mainly in the book
of Deuteronomy and in the Psalter. Here it is found frequently.
'Thou shalt love the Lord thy God with all thine heart, and with
all thy soul, and with all thy might.'[4] 'Thou shalt love the Lord
thy God, and keep his charge, and his statutes, and his judgements,
and his commandments, alway.'[5] 'What doth the Lord thy God
require of thee, but to fear the Lord thy God, to walk in his ways,
and to love him, and to serve the Lord thy God with all thy heart
and with all thy soul?'[6] All these passages are found in Deuteronomy, and many others which directly or implicitly summon men
to love God stand in that book. From the Psalter might be
quoted 'Love the Lord, all ye his saints';[7] 'ye that love the Lord,
hate evil';[8] 'I love the Lord, because he hath heard my voice
and my supplication.'[9]

No parallels to these passages can be culled from the prophets
whom we have studied. We may leave the passages from the
psalms aside, since their age cannot be discussed with confidence,
though there is a greater readiness to find considerable pre-exilic
elements in the Psalter than there was formerly. But so far as
Deuteronomy is concerned, if the common view that it was
written in the seventh century and rested on the work of the
eighth-century prophets is correct, it may well be that this demand
for love to God as the response to all the evidences of His love, and
as the spring of obedience to His will, reflects the influence of the

---

[1] Mark xii. 29 ff.   [2] Deut. vi. 5.   [3] Lev. xix. 18.
[4] Deut. vi. 5.   [5] Deut. xi. 1.   [6] Deut. x. 12.
[7] Psa. xxxi. 23 (Heb. 24). [8] Psa. xcvii. 10.   [9] Psa. cvi. 1.

eighth-century prophets. It is to be remembered, however, that the prophets sometimes used the word *know* in the sense of *love*.[1] Thus Amos says 'You only have I *known* of all the families of the earth',[2] where the sense is more than we mean by knowledge.[3] When the prophets speak of knowing God,[4] therefore, they mean something more than an intellectual knowledge of God, and think of something of the nature of love, though they do not use this term. In the great passage from the book of Micah, which, whether it is actually from Micah or not, is commonly dated early in the seventh century, at about the time when the book of Deuteronomy was most probably written, the prophetic demand for man to walk humbly with God is made.[5] This rests on a conception of the relationship of friends between God and man involving therefore mutual love, though not the love of equals. It is a love which is marked by reverence on the side of man and by grace on the side of God. Later in the same century Jeremiah can say in the name of God: 'I remember your early devotion, the love of your bridal days.'[6] While this is a metaphor of the relations between God and Israel in the ideal past, it is a metaphor which recognized that God desires the love of men. In the following century Deutero-Isaiah can refer to Abraham as the friend of God, and the word he uses for friend is lover.[7] There is therefore some reason to think that the prophets conceived of the true relationship between God and man as consisting of an intimate and enriching fellowship, into which mutual love and loyalty enter.

Here we must leave our study. It has shown us that truly prophetic qualities marked Confucius,[8] Mencius and Mo-

---

[1] Cf. H. Cohen, *Jüdische Schriften*, i, 1924, p. 311: 'So wird es verständlich, dass Erkennen im hebräischen Sprachgeiste identisch wird mit Liebe.'

[2] Amos iii. 2.

[3] Cf. what I have written in *The Biblical Doctrine of Election*, 1950, p. 53 n.: 'The sense is clearly not merely *recognized*, but *recognized as mine*, or *chosen*.' Cf. A. Neher, *Amos*, 1950, pp. 34 ff., where this verse is discussed, and where it is noted that the Jewish commentator Rashi understood it to mean *loved*, and Kimhi *chosen*.   [4] Cf., e.g., Hos. ii. 20, Jer. ix. 24, xxxi. 34.

[5] Mic. vi. 8.   [6] Jer. ii. 2 (Moffatt's rendering).   [7] Isa. xli. 8.

[8] L. Giles (*The Sayings of Confucius*, p. 7) says 'Confucius is one of the few supremely great figures in the world's history.'

tzŭ[1] as well as the prophets of Israel.[2] We have found in these spokesmen in China as in the Hebrew prophets a passion to reform men and so to reform the world, a vision of a world marked by righteousness and peace, and a sense of a mission divinely given. Amongst the Hebrew prophets there are diversities of level, and our thought has been principally of the greatest of the prophets. Amongst the Chinese Sages there were diversities of level, and here our thought has been more largely limited to the three figures who most exhibited the mark of the prophet. Even amongst these Mo-tzŭ is marked by a deeper religious quality, or at least by a stronger emphasis on religion in his teaching. Confucius was more reticent about whatever commerce with God he may have known, and as a religious influence has been less effective than as a moral and political teacher. For a time Mo-tzŭ exercised a greater influence in China than did Confucius,[3] and it seemed

---

[1] W. Corswant (*R.Th.Ph.*, N.S. xxxiv, 1946, p. 123) says of Mo-tzŭ: 'Il appartient de droit à cette élite d'hommes parfaitement intègres, courageux et désintéressés . . . qui ont consacré leur vie entière, tous leurs efforts, toutes les ressources de leur intelligence et de leur cœur aux problèmes de la morale individuelle, politique et sociale, et partant, au bien de leur pays.'

[2] Legge's extraordinary change of view about Confucius is well known. In the first edition of *The Chinese Classics*, vol. i, he said 'After long study of his character and opinions, I am unable to regard him as a great man. . . . He threw no new light on any of the questions which have a world-wide interest. He gave no impulse to religion' (Prolegomena, p. 113). Thirty years later, in the second edition, for this passage he substituted: 'The more I have studied his character and opinions, the more highly I have come to regard him. He was a very great man, and his influence has been on the whole a great benefit to the Chinese, while his teachings suggest important lessons to ourselves who profess to belong to the school of Christ' (p. 111). It is with this latter judgement that I find myself in agreement, though I would retain from the former the statement 'He gave no impulse to religion.' While I believe that he was genuinely religious, he did little to make religion vital for others. Wieger (*Histoire des Croyances religieuses*, p. 135) seems to me much less than just to Confucius when he says 'Confucius exige, quoi? . . . la charité, le dévouement? . . . oh! pas du tout.— Il exige, la *neutralité de l'esprit* et cette *froideur du cœur*.'

[3] On the various reasons suggested for his eclipse, cf. my *Submission in Suffering*, pp. 114 ff. To the suggestions there recorded may be added Wilhelm's (*A Short History of Chinese Civilization*, E.Tr., p. 173): 'too strict and ascetic, after sharing the honours with Confucianism for a time in the Chinese states, it (i.e. the teaching of Mo-tzŭ) finally fell a victim to its own excessive readiness to die'.

that the roles which they ultimately came to play would be reversed.[1] But even with Mo-tzŭ God was a remote Being rather than a living personality with Whom men might come into intimate relationship.

It is precisely here that all three of the Chinese teachers stand below all the great Hebrew prophets who have occupied our attention. To them God could not be supposed to have been merely an idea clothed with personal attributes, but One vividly conceived as a Person, with Whom men might walk and Whose voice men might hear. It is for this reason that as religious teachers they have been so much more influential than the Chinese Sages. Yet even to say this is not to depreciate the Chinese teachers. For the heritage into which they entered was less rich than that into which the Hebrew prophets entered. Behind these stood Moses and a religious inheritance which, though it had been thrown away in part by generations of indifferent drifters, had been preserved at least in part by men like Nathan and Elijah. The eighth- and seventh-century prophets did not arise suddenly out of nothing, but out of a background of religious heritage and tradition which the Chinese Sages did not have. Let them be judged in terms of their own times and conditions and let them be honoured with the honour that is their due. From the vantage point of our yet greater heritage it is easy for us to slight them. Yet when we ask what we have that we have not been given, or what we have added to the religious heritage that our children will have, we may appreciate better the high quality of all these prophetic figures, both of China and of Israel.

[1] Mencius says that in his time 'the words of Yang Chu and Mo Ti fill the country. If you listen to people's discourses throughout it, you will find that they have adopted the views either of Yang or of Mo' (*Mencius* III Part 2, ix. 9). In the following century the *Lü Shih Ch'un Ch'iu* offers testimony to the fact that 'the followers of Confucius and Mo-tzŭ, whose fame and influence are felt by all men everywhere, are innumerable' (II, iv; cf. XXV, iii. German translation in Wilhelm, *Frühling und Herbst des Lü Bu We*, 1928, pp. 24, 437), and Han-Fei-tzŭ says the schools of Confucius and of Mo-tzŭ were the two most famous schools in the country (*Han-Fei-tzŭ* l; this chapter is not included in Liao's translation so far published).

INDEX

I. Subjects

II. Modern Authors

III. References

1. BIBLICAL

MARK		LUKE		JOHN	
ix.37	114n.	x.29ff.	72n.	vi.27	114n.
xii.29ff.	141n.	xiv.26	114n.	vii.16	114n.

2. CHINESE

Date

DEC 18 2008

Demco 293-5